HOW TO ENJOY YOUR WORK & SUCCEED

C. NORTHCOTE PARKINSON
M. K. RUSTOMJI
S. A. SAPRE

VISION BOOKS
(Incorporating Orient Paperbacks)
New Delhi • Mumbai • Hyderabad

Surely there must be work to do in heaven,
Since work is the best thing on earth we know.
Lucy Larcom

www.vision**books**india.com

ISBN 81-7094-430-9

First Published 1991
Reprinted 1992, 1995, 1999, 2001, 2003, 2006, 2008

Published by
Vision Books Pvt. Ltd.
(Incorporating Orient Paperbacks & CARING imprints)
24 Feroze Gandhi Road, Lajpat Nagar III
New Delhi 110024, India.
Phone: (+91-11) 2983 6470
Fax: (+91-11) 2983 6490
E-mail: visionbk@vsnl.com

Printed at
Rashtra Rachna Printers
C-88, Ganesh Nagar, Pandav Nagar Complex,
Delhi 110092 (India).

C. Northcote Parkinson needs little introduction to his very large number of readers. He taught in universities as far apart as Illinois and Liverpool, Harvard and Malaya. He wrote the world-famous *Parkinson's Law* and many other books which have sold in millions.

M.K. Rustomji was a top executive in the Tata Engineering and Locomotive Company, TELCO, one of the largest organisations of its kind in the world, before turning to consulting and writing. His numerous books on Management remain in great demand in countries such as U.K., U.S.A., India, Spain, Japan, etc. Rustomji published twenty books in collaboration with C. Northcote Parkinson and co-authored a popular book on health with the world-famous Dr. Christian Barnard. He thrice won the Escorts Book Award for the best Management Book of the Year. He was also assigned the prestigious and path-breaking task of reorganisation and streamlining the entire administration of Andhra Pradesh. One of Rustomji's books was made into a prize winning film by the Government of India.

S.A. Sapre, was, for many years, the chief executive of one of the largest and most modern printing organisations in India. He lectured extensively and wrote a number of important books on management. Of his essay on Clement Attlee, 'The Art of Administration', Kenneth Harris, Editor of *The Observer* and author of the biography of Attlee has said: 'The essay is beyond praise, beautifully written, and full splendid insights and brilliantly selected references. It is a classic.'

☞ Comments on Parkinson-Rustomji Bestsellers

"The attraction is not only the universality of message, but also the eye-catching way in which it is presented."
Financial Times, London

"Effective and attractive . . . I am issuing instructions to have a few copies available for all the companies in our group."
J.R.D. Tata

"I have not seen anything of its kind nearly as good."
Lord Pilkington, Chairman, Pilkington Ltd.

"Excellent . . . unquestionably worthwhile." David Rockefeller

"Must for every executive." *The Times of India*

". . . most interesting and rewarding." Russi Mody,
Former Chairman, Tata Iron & Steel Co. Ltd. (TISCO)

"Scintillating — no (other) books bring out the philosophy of management half so simply." *Financial Express*

"Remarkably clever . . . should have world-wide application."
Sir Kenneth Hague, Chairman
Babcock & Wilcox Ltd., U.K.

"Most impressive." Director, Industrial Society, London

"Meant for managers at all levels — combine wisdom with clarity and simplicity." *The Economic Times.*

"We admire your initiative and the end-product that you have produced." Director General, British Institute of Management

"I am not surprised at the great success of your books."
N.A. Palkhivala

". . . contain a large number of useful hints."
S. Moolgaokar, Former Chairman
Tata Engineering & Locomotive Co. Ltd. (TELCO)

"The authors have a great knock for making ideas intelligible."
Onlooker

Contents

CHAPTER 1

Importance of objectives and details

An absent minded judge

A top ranking American judge was famous not only for his profound knowledge of law but also for his total absent mindedness. On one occasion a ticket checker approached him for his ticket while he was travelling by train; he regretted that he had forgotten to buy one. When the ticket checker respectfully said, 'Sir, could you please tell me from where you boarded the train and where you want to go?', the judge said in distress, 'The trouble is precisely that, that's exactly what I cannot recollect'. Many managements have similar problems. They do not define their objectives clearly and even if they do so, they fail to pay proper attention to details which make the achievement of the objectives possible. To be successful, managers must do the right things in the right manner. This is the basic theme of this book.

University administration in shambles

The objectives of a university are well defined. Broadly speaking, they are teaching and research. The achievement of these objectives, however, depends upon perfection in day-to-day administration. One of the main functions of the university is to conduct examinations with the utmost efficiency. Today the conduct of university examinations has become a matter of disgrace. And this has given rise to unprecedented legal disputes and in one case even the Chief Minister of a state had to resign. Very recently, a case has come to light where the examiner destroyed the answer books instead of returning them to the university. It is easy to talk of lofty ideals and objectives, but it requires unrelaxing vigilance and minute attention to details to achieve them. And very often this is what is lacking.

■ Tennessee Valley Authority

On the other hand, the failure to define objectives can be damaging. In the initial years the TVA project was in a state of chaos for want of well defined objectives. The authorities were trying to do a number of things at the same time, such as flood control, power generation, afforestation, community development, and so on. Nothing worthwhile could be achieved and there was widespread discontent about the administration of the project. Finally, President Roosevelt had to replace the administrator, Arthur Morgan, no doubt a great engineer, by David Lilienthal, a young utility lawyer.

The very first thing Lilienthal did was to specify the objective as power generation, which was pursued unwaveringly. The results were spectacular. The project came to be recognised as one of the most successful projects of its kind in the world.

■ The birth of Marks and Spencer in 1884

Marks and Spencer was started by Michael Marks in 1884 as a penny bazaar. Being an immigrant, his knowledge of English was meagre, but he had vision and practical abilities. He defined the objective of his new business as the sale of best quality goods which could be sold at a uniform price, one penny each.

And he did this very imaginatively. The goods were displayed in open baskets, so that customers themselves could choose them. The display board was worded very cleverly. 'Don't ask the price, it is a penny'. The firm grew rapidly.

■ Marks and Spencer today

Simon Marks visited America in 1924 and studied carefully the working of Sears, Roebuck and Company, the largest and the most profitable retailer in the world. Its success was primarily due to the analysis of the customer and the market, apart from innovation in many other areas.

This visit prompted Marks and Spencer to carry out a similar analysis of the home market, which showed that it was necessary to redefine the objective of their own business. Marks and Spencer defined their new objective as provision of high class clothing for the middle and lower classes at prices acceptable to them. This new objective had great social significance. In those days while the upper classes were elegantly attired, the lower classes dressed shabbily, although they too wanted to dress well. There was thus a huge market potential for quality clothing at moderate prices, which Marks and Spencer proposed to exploit.

To achieve this objective, the firm had to organise its multifarious activities, ranging from consumer analysis to planning of retail stores, with meticulous attention. Its insistence on quality control is legendary. It is said that it is extremely difficult to detect faults in the goods rejected by those who buy for Marks and Spencer.

■ God is in the details

It will be clear from the above example that it is not enough to define the objective correctly. It must be translated into action equally correctly. The goods produced for sale must be flawless and perfect. For instance, an extra pinch of salt can spoil a meal, however imaginatively the menu might have been planned. As the great architect, Mies van der Rohe, has rightly said, 'God is in the details'.

Sergiu Commission is world famous as the conductor of the Houston Symphony Orchestra in America. He is described as 'terrific' because he does not waste his musicians' time. His instructions to them are very precise. He tells them with absolute clarity what exactly he wants to hear from them at any given moment. It is the attention bestowed on details that makes his music great.

Duke of Wellington's three golden rules of management

The great Duke of Wellington has given us three golden rules of management.

First rule

'My rule always was to do the business of the day in the day'.

Second rule

'A place for every thing and every thing in its place'.

For instance, he ensured that the sick got their cots and quilts, the healthy an exact mixture of arrack and water, and the bullocks a precise speed and load.

He was renowned for his attention to detail.

Third rule

'I will get upon my horse and take a look, and then tell you'.

He believed in seeing things for himself with his own eyes. For instance, in his historic battles against Napoleon's army in Portugal and Spain, he spent several weeks riding all over the Lisbon peninsula, along with his chief engineer, who soon received from him a twenty one point memorandum along with an essay on how to hold the terrain against the impending attack by Napoleon's eagles.

Wellington, of course, was a brilliant strategist but equally important was his attention to minute but important details. And this is the secret of his resounding victories.

For instance, in the great battle at Assaye (1803) he defeated the Marathas decisively, against heavy odds. He had an army of only 7,000, one-sixth the size of the Maratha army. His cavalry was outnumbered by twenty to one, while he was equipped with only twenty-two cannons to the Maratha's hundred and more. Later he became world famous when he defeated Napoleon in the great battle at Waterloo in 1815, which proved to be a turning point in the history of Europe.

■ Routine and innovative work

Innovation plays a key role in economic development. Organisations can survive and grow only through innovation. For example, around 1925 the mail order business was replaced by retail chains, which led to a marketing revolution in America. Similarly, the introduction of airlines was a major innovation which drastically reduced the transport of passengers by steamers.

But innovation is far from easy. It requires a different type of organisation; a type of management prepared to take risks. The effect of innovation is uncertain. But innovation is successful only when it is converted into a streamlined routine. For instance, consider the introduction of airlines in place of passenger steamers. Ports were replaced by aerodromes, sailors by pilots. But the day-to-day management of airlines comprises innumerable routine operations, such as maintenance of planes and aerodromes, sale of tickets, provision of refreshments and meals on the flights, and so on. If a flight is abnormally delayed or cancelled for any reason, the passengers are justifiably very annoyed.

From the passenger's point of view, every detail is important; punctuality of flights, convenient booking facilities, prompt and courteous service by air hostesses. But the staff get bored with these routine matters.

As a result of any innovation, then the existing routine is replaced by a new one. And routine management must necessarily function with unfailing regularity like a clock in perfect order.

One of the most fundamental problems in management is how to enthuse employees to do their daily work to perfection.

Boredom of routine

■ Failure to take care of details

A few examples are given below to illustrate how a slight error of detail can lead to major problems.

■ Stalin's misplaced signature

After Russia's victory in the Second World War, Stalin began to take keen personal interest in the designing of prestigious buildings which he thought should reflect the nation's might. All architectural designs of such buildings had to have his approval. The architect for the famous Moskva Hotel had prepared two alternative designs of the front elevation, for Stalin's approval. Both designs appeared side by side on a single sheet, separated by a dividing line. This was done to make comparison at a glance easy.

But Stalin thought that it was only one single design and signed across the dividing line. It was therefore impossible to say which design was approved by Stalin and none had the courage to seek a clarification from the dictator. Ultimately, the architect made use of both designs and the hotel now sports a divided facade.

■ The mystery of the broken washroom doors

It was observed many years ago that the expenditure on repairs to washroom doors on small railway lines in the USA was mounting. This was found to be due to a minor accounting misjudgement.

It was then the practice to keep the washroom doors locked and the key was kept by the ticket agent who would give it to any passenger on request. Very often the passengers would forget to return the key and there was no alternative but to break open the door when another passenger wanted to use the washroom.

On grounds of economy, only one key was issued to the station master and he could not buy another, as that would count as capital expenditure;repairs, on the other hand, would qualify as revenue expenditure, which the station master had powers to sanction.

As a result, there was a heavy expenditure on repairs, in order to save a negligible expenditure on keys, apart from the inconvenience involved.

Treating the cost of a new key as capital expenditure was a mistake of detail, which resulted in heavy financial losses.

How an empty envelope came to be presented to the first Governor-General of India

The independence of India was proclaimed exactly at midnight (14-15 August 1947) at a special meeting of the Constituent Assembly. It was arranged that after the meeting Rajendra Prasad and Nehru would call on Mountbatten and invite him to be the first constitutional Governor-General of India.

At the midnight hour, Mountbatten was sitting at his desk in his study, serenely awaiting Prasad and Nehru. At a simple ceremony the formalities were completed and Mountbatten accepted the invitation to be Governor-General. Nehru then handed over to him a large and carefully addressed envelope, saying, 'May I submit to you the portfolios of the new cabinet.'

After Prasad and Nehru had left, Mountbatten opened the envelope with great curiosity to see the names of the new ministers. To his great surprise, the envelope was empty. Somebody had overlooked a very important detail.

■ Attention to small details can produce excellent results

These illustrations show how failure to take care of apparently small matters can give rise to big problems. On the other hand, proper attention to details can produce excellent results as will be seen from the following cases

How a government office was made beautiful

Government offices are seldom maintained in an orderly way. They are often dusty and depressing. In one such office, a newly appointed lady stenographer was asked to look after the work of the personal assistant to the officer, who had suddenly proceeded on leave.

The stenographer had an eye for elegance, cleanliness, and order. She was aghast to see the mess in the officer's chamber. The officer's table was always covered with dust and cluttered with things. The pencils were never properly sharpened. The files were piled up in a disorderly fashion. The young secretary ensured that the table was kept spotlessly clean. She started keeping a few fresh and fragrant flowers on the table. Pencils were regularly sharpened and neatly kept. The files were classified and systematically arranged. A neatly typed note indicating the meetings and appointments for the day was regularly placed on the table. All these things were very minor in themselves but their total impact was great. The chamber bore a new appearance, reflecting freshness and elegance. It greatly renewed the officer's own interest in his work, as it was a delight to work in such pleasant surroundings.

■ Arranging waistcoats in a display room

A renowned French artist, Fernand Leger, has given a graphic description of a display artist arranging waistcoats with meticulous care in a small display room.

'The man had seventeen waistcoats to arrange in his window, with as many sets of cufflinks and neckties surrounding them. He spent about eleven minutes on each; we timed him. We left, tired out, after the sixth item. We had been there for one full hour in front of him as he would come out to see the effect after having shifted these items by one millimeter. Each time he came out, he was so absorbed that he did not even see us. With the dexterity of a fitter, he arranged his spectacles brow wrinkled, eyes fixed, as if his whole life depended on it.'

This is another vivid illustration of the statement that God is in the details.

How Prime Minister Attlee paid attention to important details

Harold Wilson, who was a minister in Attlee's cabinet, and who later became Prime Minister of England himself, has said that Attlee brought great clarity of mind to matters great and small.

As Prime Minister he had all the secretarial assistance but would often type out his own important letters and quite often, write secret letters in his own hand. In exceptional cases, he would himself seal such letters as the following instance shows.

In 1948 an Act providing the most comprehensive system of social security was introduced in the U.K. Attlee made a non-political broadcast to give this new Social Service Scheme a good start.

But at the same time, Aneurin Bevan, the Minister for Health, who was directly concerned with the scheme, launched a vicious attack on the Tories condemning them as lower than vermin.

This was a very unwise speech, inappropriate for an occasion when the nation as a whole was expected to rejoice. It intensified inter-party conflict which assumed

Typing one's own secret documents

ugly proportions. Attlee then wrote a very persuasive letter to Bevan in his own hand in order to ensure secrecy, asking him to be careful in future. To leave no scope for leakage, he marked the outer envelope 'Strictly Personal' and the inner envelope was inscribed, 'To be opened by the Minister only. No action till he calls for his papers'.

Attlee was an ideal Prime Minister in several ways. The development of the atom bomb during his office was such a closely guarded secret that no one (with the exception of four or five persons) had any idea that such a major project was under way. Attlee had no temptations. He did not seek publicity. He never used three words where one would do. He was committed to his well-defined objectives and worked most systematically to attain them.

Just-in-time system (JIT system)

The credit for developing and perfecting this revolutionary production system goes to Toyota. It is the culmination of very hard work extended over a period of twenty-five years. The essence of the system lies in the minutest attention given to all details.

- The system aims at the following results:
- Goods produced and delivered just in time for sales.
- Sub-assemblies assembled just in time into finished goods.
- Parts fabricated just in time to go into sub-assemblies.
- Materials transformed just in time into fabricated parts.

It is not just an inventory control system which aims at reducing the capital locked up in materials, reducing the size of warehouses and facilitating accounting and physical inventory control. The system is far more comprehensive as the following illustration shows.

■ Cutting set-up time

In 1971 Toyota launched a campaign to cut set-up time. It then took an hour to set up 800-ton presses used for manufacturing automobile hoods and fenders. Within five years the time was reduced to 12 minutes. In fact, Japanese firms are now planning to reduce set-up time to zero! Each machine will be designed for one job alone and all that the worker has to do is to load and unload.

The comparative labour productivity of Japanese and American automobile factories is shown below:

	Japanese Firm	American Firm
Man per day per unit	1:1	2.5:1

Manufacturing labour productivity depends on the perfect coordination of a multitude of details. Toyota is the largest manufacturer of automobiles in Japan today.

Perhaps the difficulties in perfecting such an extremely complex JIT system will be better appreciated from the following account of shortages of nails in Soviet Russia.

Why there were shortages of nails in Soviet Russia

When Gosplan, the State Planning Board, specified the production of nails in terms of weight, factories produced only large nails to meet the target. When this mistake came to light, the target was fixed in terms of the number of nails. But then the factories concentrated on the production of only very small nails to meet the target. Shortages merely shifted from one kind to the other.

■ The Japanese passion for precision

The Japanese have a fixation for statistical information. They count and calculate everything endlessly. When they were building the largest oil tanker in the world, *Idemitsu Maru,* weighing 300,000 tons, the precision in construction was such that by merely consulting the record of expenditures and the work plan, it was possible to ascertain accurately the daily progress in the shipyard.

■ Small can be revolutionary

By 1960 Japan had an abundance of motor cars but the existing network of roads was totally inadequate. The roads were narrow with many lanes and bylanes. Accidents were mounting at an alarming rate, particularly at night. Roads cannot be widened or new roads constructed within a short period. This is essentially a long term task.

At this juncture a young Japanese, Tamon Iwasa, came up with a simple solution. He redesigned the traditional highway reflector in such a way that the headlights of oncoming cars could be seen from a distance from any direction. The government installed thousands of these reflectors and the accident rate came down sharply.

CHAPTER 2

On making work interesting

Reasons for distaste for work

n this chapter we propose to discuss the following topics:

I. How an executive should deal with the problem of excessive workload.

II. How he can deal with monotonous and boring work

III. How he can enthuse his subordinates to produce better work.

Dealing with excessive work

There are various ways in which the problem of excessive work can be successfully dealt with.

Eliminate unnecessary work

Very often executives do a good deal of work which is, in fact, unnecessary. A classic illustration is provided by Ian Hamilton who reduced his anticipated workload of 36 hours a day to a mere 6 hours.

How a military officer reduced his workload from 36 hours a day to only 6 hours a day

The following is an extract from Ian Hamilton's book:

'In 1896 I was Deputy Quartermaster-General at Simla; then, perhaps still, one of the hardest worked billets in Asia. After a long office day I used to get back home to dinner, pursued by a pile of files three to four feet high. The Quartermaster-General, my boss, was a clever, delightful work-glutton. So we sweated and ran together for a while a neck and neck race with our piles of files, but I was the younger and he was the first to be ordered off by the doctors to Europe. Then I, at the age of forty-three, stepped into his shoes and became officiating Quartermaster-General in India. Unluckily, the Government at that moment was in a very stingy mood. They refused to provide pay to fill the post I was vacating and Sir George White, the Commander-in-Chief, asked me to duplicate myself and do the double work. My heart sank, but there was nothing for it but to have a try. The day came; the Quartermaster-General went home and with him went the whole of his share of the work. As for my own share, the hard twelve hours' task melted by some magic into the Socialist's dream of a six hours day. How was that? Because, when a question came up from one of the Departments, I had been forced to compose a long minute upon it, explaining the case, putting my own views, and endeavoring to persuade the Quartermaster-General to accept them. He was a highly conscientious man and if he differed from me he liked to put on record his reasons -- several pages of reasons. Or, if he agreed with me, still he liked to agree in his own words and to "put them on record". Now, when I became Quartermaster-General and Deputy Quartermaster-General rolled into one I studied the case as formerly, but there my work ended: I had not to persuade my own subordinates, I had no superior except the Commander-in-Chief, who was delighted to be left alone. I just gave the order, quite a simple matter, unless a man's afraid. "Yes", I said, or "No."

■ Delegate

There is always scope for delegation of some work to subordinates. Appropriate delegation is in fact the key to effective management. A good executive trusts his subordinates, gives them necessary guidance and does not unnecessarily interfere in their work. Subordinates develop best in such an atmosphere. The best way to train people is to give them responsible work. Adequate delegation was the basis of British administration in India which, it is said, enabled one Englishman to do the work of twenty Frenchmen!

Simplify and standardise

It is useful to examine whether any particular work can be simplified and standardised. For instance, when Mountbatten began his work as Viceroy, he had to interview a large number of leaders. He arranged the interviews in such a way that there was an interval of fifteen minutes between interviews. In this interval Mountbatten dictated a resume of the last discussion. These notes were serially numbered and immediately circulated to the concerned officials. This method ensured utmost accuracy in preparing the minutes as they were dictated immediately after the interview.

In government offices the normal practice is for the staff to put up a note for the officer's approval and a draft reply is prepared on approval of the note. One officer changed this usual procedure and instructed that no note was required in routine matters and that a draft reply should be submitted straightaway. This saved a good deal of time of both the officer and the staff.

Plan your work

The importance of planning is not sufficiently recognised. Busy executives often think that the nature of their work is such that no planning is possible or that they have no time for planning. President Nixon's daily routine was meticulously planned. The case of Frank Bettger, regarded at one time as one of America's top five salesmen, deserves to be mentioned. Early in his career he realised the importance of planning and set aside Saturday mornings for this purpose calling it 'self-organisation day'. The results were most encouraging. As he could do far more and better work as a result of planning, his enthusiasm for work increased from week to week. And enthusiasm is, as he says, the key to success.

Eliminate time-wasters

Executives who complain of overwork are often not aware of the time and energy they just fritter away. These time-wasters are telephone interruptions, drop-in-visitors, unduly prolonged meetings, flow of excessive information, an untidy desk, unsystematic habits of work and wrong priorities. A record, properly maintained for a few days, can suggest how to reduce wastage of time as explained fully in Chapter 5.

■ Practice continuously

An executive can improve his performance by constant practice. He can learn to concentrate effectively and improve his communication skills, written and oral, as well as his decision-making capacity. His motto should be: The day's work must be done during the day.

President Richard Nixon's daily routine

Nixon worked in the traditional fashion. He preferred working alone and planning on paper. He expected all options to be clearly spelt out, with their advantages and disadvantages. He required plenty of time to read, reflect, and decide. He disliked meetings and was a great believer in paper work. He thought that ideas were best presented on paper; not through discussion.

His daily routine was worked out with great care. The day was divided into half-hour segments and plenty of time was reserved for thinking. All requests for appointments were subjected to close scrutiny. It was not easy to get an appointment and visitors had to complete their business within the allotted time.

The White House Staff met daily at 7.30 a.m. to identify problems and priorities for the day. At 8.30 a.m. top advisers would further scrutinise the report before presenting it to the President.

Precisely at 9.00 a.m. the President would arrive at the office and start work in right earnest.

Earlier, at 7.45 a.m., the President would receive, at his residence, a notebook, 'The President's Daily News Briefing', which kept him in touch with all important developments. Nixon had no trust in newspapers, which he never read. So, too, he never watched TV.

■ Procrastination and brooding

A good deal of time is often wasted as a result of procrastination even in simple matters. Similarly, brooding seriously impairs the capacity for work. It is debilitating. Prime Minister Attlee had perfected the art of decision-making.

Prime Minister Attlee as decision-maker par excellence

This is how he managed his work.

'By not worrying, clearing off every day's job before the end of the day. You take a decision and then have done with it. No good to keep on asking yourself if you have done the right thing. It gets you nowhere'.

'What one needs in a Cabinet Minister is decisiveness and a sense of priorities, ability to make up his mind. He must be able to select and absorb the necessary amount of information and not cumber his mind with a whole lot of unnecessary stuff. The fellow who goes wrong is the laborious fellow who reads everything in great detail and is quite unable to get any sense of priorities'.

■ Challenging work

A challenge should be looked upon as an opportunity to learn something new and achieve something remarkable. An individual develops himself best when he faces challenging situations. When he meets a challenge successfully, it strengthens his self-confidence and enhances his self-respect. In such situations, work becomes a stimulating and enjoyable activity. When, for instance, a student solves a difficult mathematical problem, he wants to tackle an even more difficult one.

■ Adequate relaxation

The executive must learn to relax adequately. E.E.H. Edye was a remarkable district collector who would always find time for golf, shooting or polo. As a result, his thinking was always clear and vigorous and his appetite for work enormous. He reached his decisions swiftly and in a detached manner.

A different type of work as relaxation

A different type of work best suited to one's talent and aptitude can be excellent and invigorating relaxation. Walter Leaf, an eminent banker, was also a great classical scholar. But he kept his two identities in separate watertight compartments. It was believed that there were two different experts of the same name. His banking friends did not know that he was also a classical scholar. Similarly, the scholars had no idea that their colleague was also an expert banker. The facts came to light when both scholars and bankers got together at his funeral.

Some of the British ICS Officers were not only able and devoted administrators but also great scholars. Grierson was one such scholar-administrator who completed his lifelong study *Linguistic Survey of India* at the age of 78. It is a monumental work, dealing with 180 Indian languages and 480 dialects.

Monotonous nature of work

In the interest of efficiency, work in a factory or office is minutely subdivided and reduced to simple specialised operations. Everything is standardised; methods, tools and materials. The worker himself becomes a mere cog in a vast and complicated machinery. He remains preoccupied with one small insignificant operation. As a result the work becomes intensely boring and meaningless. There is no scope for his abilities as a human being and the work gets indifferently performed.

The problem is exceedingly complex and a wide variety of solutions have been suggested which are briefly discussed here.

Importance of routine work

It is necessary to bear in mind that routine work is not only not meaningless but is something essential from every point of view, as fully explained in Chapter I. For example, the gangman who maintains the railway track, performs an essential task. His negligence can lead to a serious railway accident.

Routine work can be made beautiful

The Japanese have perfected this art. They beautify everything. They really believe that 'Cleanliness is next to Godliness' and ensure utmost cleanliness everywhere. The Japanese are always immaculately dressed and their shirts are, at any time of the day, as white as if fresh from the laundry. Even taxi drivers and gardeners use white handgloves. Cars have their chromium gleaming. When a customer enters a restaurant, he is given a hot face towel to wipe his face and feel refreshed. Every taxi driver has a vase in front of him with fresh flowers. A sandwich is a work of art, with a design and a colour scheme. Even rubbish is beautifully packed in Japan.

Even garbage is well packed in Japan

Tea drinking is a commonplace activity elsewhere but the Japanese have developed it into a fine art—the Tea Ceremony.

The tea ceremony : An exercise in elegance

The tea ceremony may be regarded as a distinctive feature of Japanese culture. The original rules for the ceremony are laid down in seven volumes which deal with its every aspect in a thorough fashion. The basic idea is that there is a best way of serving tea, of furnishing a tea room, making the charcoal fire glow. The underlying principle is that of stage art. It is not the role that makes a great actor but the way he plays it.

A brief description of the ceremony can best be given in the words of Jean-Claude Courdy, author of *The Japanese.* 'The Japanese have created around this myth a ritual evocative of peace, relaxation, and frankness among those who drink tea together.... The tea is prepared in silence, in accordance with certain detailed and immutable gestures. It is drunk religiously, the participants having turned their bowls around three times before bringing them to their lips. The tea ceremony is an opportunity for the attainment of inner concentration, in preparation for the harmony which must reign between friends who meet, or between partners who must discuss'.

The soul of the tea ceremony, it is said, lies in a moment of relief snatched from the pressure of work.

For our purpose the lesson is that the tea ceremony shows how even ordinary work can be made meaningful, beautiful and most satisfying.

■ Work can be play

An eminent Dutch historian has advanced a novel thesis that play is all-pervading in human life. Even business assumes the form of a game. In support of this contention he quotes a well-known industrialist as saying:

'Ever since I first entered business it has been a race between the technicians and the sales department. One tried to produce so much that the sales department would never be able to sell it, while the other tried to sell so much that the technicians would never be able to keep pace. This race has always continued; sometimes one is ahead, sometimes the other. Neither my brother nor I have regarded business as a task, but always as a game, the spirit of which it has been our constant endeavor to implant into the younger staff.'

In some Japanese restaurants the chefs have turned the cutting of food into an art form. When they are cooking vegetables, they toss them skilfully into the air.

■ It is useful to start an inner game

It is said that waiters in big restaurants turn out to be good judges of men, their behaviour, their attitudes and expectations. The reason is that while they are doing their work, they are also observing them, talking to them and listening to their gossip. Watching people, thus becomes for them an interesting hobby. And this makes work itself more interesting. These waiters take great pride in serving celebrities like famous film actresses.

While one is doing some routine work, the mind can be engaged in some other important activity. An interesting case is that of an English compositor who developed the mathematics of composing in Sanskrit at the Oxford University Press in 1849 where the Rig Veda was being printed under the editorship of Max Muller. What is noteworthy is that the compositor did not know a word of Sanskrit.

Prime Minister, Clement Attlee always doodled in colour pencil, even in the midst of stormy cabinet meetings. These doodles were collected by his private secretaries as a precious gift. Jinnah was also fond of doodling. Attlee's doodles were relatively simple, mostly elongated circles, but Jinnah's were very complicated and elaborate. It is said that his doodles reflected power and glory.

In fact this idea has been developed into a sort of a new technique by Tim Gallwey who has established the Inner Game Corporation for making routine jobs interesting, with the introduction of an inner game in the job itself. The Inner Game is described as the game of the future by Archie McGill, former head of AT & T's Advanced Information Systems.

Inner Game for Telephone Operators: A New Technique

Timothy Gallwey was captain of the Harvard Tennis Team. His book, *The Inner Game of Tennis*, proved to be a great success and his methods of teaching are extended to many fields such as skiing and music.

The American Telegraph and Telephone Company was facing a serious problem as the telephone operators could not cope with the stress of answering over 700 enquiries every day; a rather unpleasant task as most of the enquiries were in the nature of complaints. AT & T invited Tim Gallwey's Inner Game Corporation to study the problem and suggest a remedy.

His suggestion is briefly described below. The operators were instructed to do the following mental exercises:

- To listen carefully and imagine what each caller looked like.
- To assess the quality in the callers voices: warmth, irritation, vitality, sexiness, etc. on a scale ranging from 0-10.

To avoid boredom, imagine what a caller looks like

- To observe how the tone changed as the telephone talk progressed. A caller might start angrily but cool down as the matter was explained to him. The change was to be noted (mentally) on the scale.

The results may be briefly summarised as follows:

- The work became less monotonous and the additional task, an enjoyable game.
- The operators became more intimately involved in the work.

- They were able to deal with the enquiries in a more humane fashion, which in turn evoked a favorable response from the callers.
- It was possible for them to assess the effectiveness of their approach on the basis of the change in the caller's tone. For instance, if an angry and embittered caller spoke affably towards the end, it was a most rewarding experience.

There are thus innumerable ways of making routine work interesting.

■ It is useful to introduce a ritual in the work schedule

The Japanese are very imaginative and are always thinking of ways of creating, developing, and sustaining people's interest in daily work. Towards this end they have introduced a ritual in their factories. The day begins with some exercise, accompanied by music, and a company song on the following lines:

For the building of a new Japan
Let us put our mind and strength together.

A noted author has introduced a ritual in his daily work. He cleans his own writing table and arranges his books and files, before starting work every morning. And he says he enjoys the ritual which has also improved the quality of his work. He can now concentrate more effectively.

■ It is a pleasure to work in a friendly group

Work in factories and offices becomes a social activity as people work in groups or teams. Everyone wants friends. Even repetitive, monotonous, and hasty work can be a source of joy, if the group atmosphere is friendly and affectionate. The quest for fellowship is a basic human requirement.

How six girls in a slaughterhouse worked joyfully in dirty conditions

These girls were working in a slaughterhouse cleaning the internal organs and intestines of slaughtered pigs in a very depressing atmosphere. They had to work in the basement, which was always very hot, humid, and uncomfortable.

The floor was always covered with blood and the contents of pigs' intestines and the whole place stank dreadfully. A new medical officer was horrified by this spectacle and ordered that the young girls be given some decent work elsewhere. The management had to comply with this directive and planned to send these girls to different sections for some clean work such as filing, despatching etc.

But the girls raised a hue and cry. They demanded to know why they were going to be transferred when they were doing an excellent job. Their protest was so strong and persistent that the management had to withdraw the order.

The girls loved their 'dirty' work for various reasons. First and foremost, they had formed a very happy working group. They had become intimate friends. The whole day, while working, they were also talking, singing, telling stories, discussing gossip, pictures and fashions. The social atmosphere was so congenial that they were unmindful of the poor working conditions. Secondly they took pride in their work, which they considered to be highly skilled. Thirdly, the supervisor was a model supervisor who never tried to dominate them. Whenever the girls did a fine piece of work, he warmly praised them. If they had any difficulties, he guided and assisted them readily. In a sense he was their teacher. They admired and respected him.

■ Enthusing subordinates

■ Set the pace

The executive has to set the pace of work himself. If he is working with genuine enthusiasm, his subordinates will do likewise. Enthusiasm is infectious. If, on the other hand, the executive is himself indifferent in his work, the subordinates cannot be expected to be careful and enthusiastic.

It is rightly said that the distance between the leader and the average follower is constant. If the leader accelerates his pace, so do the followers.

Boss must set an example

■ Insist on high standards

The leader must clearly define the objectives to be achieved and insist on high standards of performance. It must be, time and again, impressed on the subordinates that their work is important. The survival and growth of the firm depends on their performance. And finally their job itself depends on their work, for if productivity declines sharply, the firm may have to be closed.

■ Appreciate the work of subordinates

Subordinates must be informed from time to time, how they are doing. It is said that practice makes a man perfect. But psychologists point out that practice without zeal is of no consequence, but if the rewards of practice are known, it may well lead to perfection. Appreciation of good work enhances self-respect, and this in turn improves performance. On the other hand, if the performance is not upto expectations, the reasons for unsatisfactory performance must be ascertained and the subordinates assisted, guided and encouraged to improve their work. In exceptional cases, discipline may have to be enforced.

■ Provide feedback information

Feedback enables an individual to improve his work. Emery Air Freight in America had considerable difficulty in improving the performance of its drivers. Industrial engineers could not provide any useful guidance. But when the drivers were informed of the calls they had actually made as against the number of calls they had planned to make, they started adjusting their pace of work and achieved the target.

■ Be accessible

Some supervisors are reluctant to see and talk to their subordinates. This creates a barrier between them. If the executive is accessible even when he is otherwise busy, the subordinate naturally respects him and addresses himself to his own work with renewed enthusiasm. This gives him the confidence that if at any time he has a problem he can seek guidance from his boss, who is there to protect him from errors. The Japanese executive will see his people readily, without keeping them waiting, although he may ask visitors to wait.

■ Encourage subordinates to participate

It is essential that subordinates are consulted and encouraged to put forth their suggestions. The Japanese believe that the person who is regularly doing a particular type of work is the real expert as far as that job is concerned. Decisions reached in consultation with the subordinates can be more practicable and would be carried out effectively. Participation thus improves team work.

IBM engineers finalise their designs in consultation with the group of workers who will eventually be responsible for the manufacturing activity.

The Viceroyalty of India was the biggest office in the world. Lord Wavell was a failure as Viceroy and was dismissed, while his successor, Mountbatten, was eminently successful. Mountbatten encouraged participation while Wavell shunned it.

Wavell and Mountbatten : Failure and triumph

It is an essential part of the art of administration to make the fullest possible use of the talent of one's subordinates. V.P. Menon occupied an important position as constitutional adviser to the Viceroy. He was a genius in constitutional matters and a diplomat *par excellence*. But Wavell had no faith in him and probably never even saw him.

On the contrary, Mountbatten realised quickly that Menon could be of great help to him. He would see him alone, picking his brains to make use of his ideas. Mountbatten has recorded that he was greatly influenced in planning his negotiations with V.P. Menon's ideas.

Mountbatten firmly believed in the 'sovereignty of discussion'. To him, it was the best method of uncovering snags and finding appropriate solutions.

Where Wavell proved to be a dismal failure, Mountbatten triumphed.

■ Look at mistakes in the proper light

A good executive looks upon mistakes as a means of understanding his subordinates and as a means of educating them. He is also aware that mistakes may be the result of imperfections in the organisation or his failure to give clear instructions. He does not, therefore, try to fix responsibility and impose punishment for every mistake noticed. He first rectifies the mistake and then analyses it for future guidance. This is a very healthy approach. People are then encouraged to accept responsibility, and their advancement is not arrested on account of small mistakes and errors.

How the Chief Secretary saved his Under Secretary

H.V.R. Iyengar, who rose to great eminence and became Governor of the Reserve Bank of India, started his career as Under Secretary in the Bombay Secretariat. His office once put up for his signature, a reminder to the Collector of West Khandesh, who did not care to reply despite several reminders. Iyengar was greatly annoyed that such a highly placed officer should ignore as many as eighteen reminders from the government. Instead of signing an additional reminder, he wrote a very curt letter to him asking for an immediate reply.

Later in the afternoon, he mentioned this incident to a senior colleague, who told him that such a letter could be sent only over the signature of the Chief Secretary. Iyengar rushed back to his office to withdraw the letter but it had already been despatched.

He then sent the file to the Chief Secretary for information. Next morning he received the file back from the Chief Secretary along with a confidential letter drawing his attention to the relevant rules. But what was more important, the Chief Secretary himself wrote another letter to the Collector saying, 'In continuation of the letter which I asked my Under Secretary to write to you earlier today...'

Iyengar has said, 'My attitude to the Chief Secretary became one of both admiration and gratitude, and therefore, I took particular care to see that I did not let him down.' The Chief Secretary on his part placed such great faith in him that during the last four weeks of his stay as Chief Secretary he asked Iyengar to look after his routine work. In his farewell address, the Chief Secretary made a special mention of Iyengar's assistance to him.

This is the art of administration at its best.

■ Rapport is the key

Rapport is the key to the morale of a group. A good executive develops rapport with his people, that is, mutual understanding and confidence. Then the executive's enthusiasm filters all the way downwards through the organisation and people work in tune with the boss. In such a set-up employees are eager to see the boss, while in a poorly run organisation they try to avoid him.

CHAPTER 3

Redesigning jobs and organisations

■ Alienation

Alienation is a major problem in an industrial organisation in any society, communist or capitalist. Work needs to be streamlined in the interest of efficiency, but in the process it may become monotonous and uninteresting. It may leave no scope for individual initiative and creativity. Such soulless work cripples man's spirit. He hates it intensely. One of the basic problems in industry is how to redesign work to suit a man's dignity, so that it becomes meaningful and enriches his personality.

The anguish of a factory worker

A sensitive worker has expressed his anguish in the following words:

'It is probably wrong to expect factories to be other than what they are. After all, they are built to house machines, not men. Inside a factory, it soon becomes obvious that steel brought to life by electricity takes precedence over flesh and blood.... Machines have become as much like men as men have become like machines. They pulsate with life, while man becomes the robot. There is a premonition of man losing control, an awareness of doom.

■ Meaningful work

Organisational theorists have proposed a number of remedies for making work meaningful which will be discussed in this chapter.

Restructuring of jobs

Job rotation

Job enlargement
Job enrichment
Flexi-time system
Workers' participation in management
Quality circles
The quality of working life and major reorganisation of factories.

Restructuring of jobs

Job rotation

The concept of job rotation is very simple. Employees are periodically rotated from one job to another similar or equivalent job. For instance, the ledger clerk in a bank may work as a cashier. A clerk working in the stores department of a factory may be sent to the time-keeping department.

Job enlargement

This is grouping together tasks of similar nature such as typing, filing and despatching. The typist can do all these. Such restructuring is horizontal in character. In a co-operative society, for instance, work was allotted to the staff on a

Job enlargement

functional basis, such as correspondence, maintenance, billing for the entire colony, etc. Under the new arrangement one person was made responsible for all these functions for a small group of flats.

■ Job enrichment

This is the addition of a more difficult, more responsible component of work to an existing job.

IBM is well-known for this type of restructuring of jobs. Once Thomas J. Watson, Sr., the founder of IBM, observed that a lady operator was sitting idly at her machine as the machine was to be set up for a new job by the set-up man. When Watson asked her, 'Couldn't you do it yourself?' She said, 'Of course, but the rules do not permit it.' Watson considered the matter carefully and machine setting was added to the work of machine operators. All operators were given the necessary training. Later, inspection of the finished product was also entrusted to the operator. This is one of the secrets of IBM's outstanding performance.

In a large European chemical plant, it was found that although salesmen were paid very well, sales were dwindling. It was therefore decided to give greater autonomy to them and periodic reports from them were discontinued. They were given the freedom to plan their own work and fix the frequency of their visits to customers. They were also given freer access to the technical departments and they were expected to deal with customer complaints themselves. The job was thus greatly enriched. It became more interesting as well as more challenging.

The results were very encouraging. Sales rose by 19 per cent compared with the same period in the preceding year, while the control group registered a decrease of 5 per cent over the same period.

■ Flexi-time system

Under this system, working hours are classified into two categories:

(1) Common hours when all employees must be present,
say, 10 a.m.– 2 p.m.

(2) Optional hours, say, 8 a.m. - 10 a.m.
and 2 p.m.–8 p.m.

The following conditions are imposed:

(a) Every employee must complete the prescribed number of hours per week/month.

(b) No one should exceed a certain length of working day, say, 10 hours.

The scheme was first introduced in Switzerland and it is now adopted in many other countries.

Under this arrangement, the individual can plan his work schedule to suit his convenience, taking into consideration transport availability, family needs, and personal convenience. On the other hand, the organisation's work could suffer to some extent.

■ Worker's participation in management

■ The Hawthorne investigations

These pioneering investigations were carried out in the Hawthorne Works near Chicago (USA) of the Western Electric Company from 1927 to 1932.

The purpose of the investigations was to find out what factors affect the morale of workers and mould their attitude towards work. The findings of these investigations have profoundly altered our understanding of the social organisation of an enterprise.

One of the experiments -- The First Relay Assembly Test Room Experiment -- was found to be particularly revealing. In this experiment, the variations in the output of a group of five girls assembling a small telephone part were studied under different conditions. From time to time many changes in working hours, rest, pauses, etc., were made. A five-day week was introduced. Lunch was also provided free of cost.

It was subsequently decided to withdraw the various concessions given and to restore the original conditions of work. It was expected that the withdrawal of concessions would lead to resentment and result in the fall of output. But surprisingly enough, the daily and weekly output registered a record high level.

Briefly, what had happened was that there had been a remarkable change in the attitude of this group. The girls were always consulted by the social scientists before any change was made. At first the girls were shy, hesitant, and suspicious, but gradually their attitude changed. They became more confident. They came out with suggestions freely. These suggestions were considered sympathetically. The girls thus started participating in the experiment and gradually identified themselves with the experiment. For the first time it was clearly established that participation can have a healthy impact on human behaviour and performance.

A number of research projects on participation, subsequently carried out, have confirmed these findings. Satisfaction in work is enhanced if workers are allowed to participate in the decision-making process.

■ The importance of participation

The importance of workers' participation in management was conclusively brought out by the Hawthorne investigations nearly fifty years ago. The basic idea is simple. Workers are important partners, collaborators in an enterprise. They will take pride and pleasure in shaping the policies and decisions

Importance of workers' participation

(Important partners)

affecting their enterprise. They possess the intelligence, knowledge and understanding needed for the purpose

Gandhiji's concept of trusteeship

Gandhiji had clearly foreseen the insoluble problems that would arise as a result of collective bargaining, which promotes discontent, selfishness, and unending strife. He advocated a new theory of management based on the concept of trusteeship. According to him, labour and capital (management) should act as trustees of the society. Both should enjoy equality of status, equality of power in the management of the enterprise and have equal representation on all forums conducting the affairs of the enterprise. This philosophy, however, did not work in practice, particularly because it ignores the harsh economic and social realities and the complexities of managing an enterprise in rapidly changing technological and economic conditions.

■ Workers' participation in the Electronics Corporation of India Ltd.

The corporation was registered in 1967. It manufactures a wide range of electronic components, instruments and systems.

As on 31 March 1978, the capital invested amounted to Rs.16 crores. The number of persons employed was 6,437. The turnover (sales) came to about Rs.28 crores in 1977-78. From 1973-74 onwards the profits were declining and in the year 1977-78 a loss of Rs.105 lakhs was incurred.

Organisational structure

The board of directors is appointed by the President of India, who is the sole shareholder. The board consists of a chairman, a full-time managing director and seven other part-time members. The Managing Director is assisted by a General Manager and twelve group heads in charge of production, finance and marketing. There is a separate Policy and Planning Committee which makes important decisions regarding manpower, capital investment, and so on. It is the function of the Executive Committee to implement these decisions. The Industrial

Relations Committee deals with recruitment, promotion, wage structure and other personnel matters. The seventeen production divisions are placed under six major groups.

Employees' union

The Electronics Corporation of India Union, which was formed in 1967, was recognised by the management in 1968. 86% of the workers are members of this union. There is no other employees' union in the company. The union has been provided with facilities like office accommodation, furniture, and telephone. The office-bearers are allowed time-off of 48 hours per month for attending to union work. The union subscription is 50p per month, which is deducted from the pay and made over to the union.

Industrial relations

The company has a good record of industrial relations. The percentage of man-days lost during a period of twelve years (1967-79) is only 0.11 per cent. Most of the disputes were settled through conciliation.

Three-tier participative mechanism

A three-tier system as shown below was introduced in 1975 with a view to securing workers' participation in management.

Sectional Production Committees
Divisional Production Committees
Apex Committees.

Their working is briefly described below.

Sectional Production Committees

Each division is divided into a suitable number of production units and each unit has a separate Sectional Production Committee. There are in all 29 such committees. The head of the committee is called the convenor, who presides over the meetings. He is a senior officer of the corporation. The management is represented by supervisors, whose number varies according to the size of the section. The workers' representatives are restricted to 10 per cent of the strength of the section, subject to a maximum of 8. They are appointed by the management on the basis of seniority. The committees meet once every month generally before the 10th, for not more than two hours.

Functions of the Sectional Production Committee

Its main functions are:

(a) review of monthly achievements against the targets fixed;

(b) making suggestions to the Divisional Production Committee for changes in working schedules, and suggestions for improving individual and team performance;

(c) making suggestions regarding technological improvements, safety and similar matters.

The overall objective is to improve productivity.

Divisional Production Committee

The committee is chaired by the head of the division who is also the convenor. Senior officers representing all the Sectional Production Committees are members of the Divisional Production Committee. There is one workers' representative from each of the Sectional Production Committees, who is nominated according to seniority.

Functions of the Divisional Production Committee

The functions are broadly similar to those of the Sectional Production Committees, namely, review of plans, fulfilment of production targets, and so on. It makes suggestions for improvement in the working of different sections. It considers the representations received from the Sectional Production Committees and determines the action to be taken.

Apex Committee

This Committee is headed by the Managing Director. It has three more management representatives and the union nominates two representatives. The Committee reviews the working of the Sectional and Divisional Production Committees. It is supposed to meet once in two months.

Final assessment

On the basis of the data available it cannot be said definitely whether the scheme has been a success or a failure. According to management representatives the production committees had no impact on productivity. They neither improved the working atmosphere, nor encouraged team spirit and self-discipline. This view is supported by the declining trend of profits, but again this is not conclusive. Profits are affected by a multiplicity of factors, all of which cannot be controlled by the participative mechanism. The workers' representatives, however, think differently. In their opinion the scheme had a wholesome impact on the working of the corporation. Considering the fact that the scheme has been in operation for a number of years, on balance, it can be said to have served some useful purpose. Very often such participative forums do not survive that long.

Self-management in Yugoslavia

Social ownership of means of production

In Yugoslavia factories, mines, and other state enterprises are managed by their working staffs themselves. This is self-management. The system may be very briefly described as follows.

It consists of the workers' council, the management board and the director. Members of the workers' council are elected by the workers themselves. The council enjoys wide-ranging powers. The management board is the executive organ of the enterprise. Its members are elected by the workers' council. The Director is the Chief Executive Officer, who is recruited through open competition. Trade unions act as watchdogs at the enterprise level.

Evaluation

On the whole the system has so far worked well. Jan Tinbergen (Nobel laureate in economics) has said: 'A rate of growth of per capita real income of about 6 per cent, together with a considerable degree of democracy in the everyday environment of the mass of producers, is not easily found elsewhere.'

Deficiencies of the Yugoslav system

This is not to say that the scheme has attained perfection. There is not, and there cannot be, any scheme for workers' participation which can be said to be 100 per cent successful. The following major deficiencies have been pointed out in a recent study by Alec Nove:

(a)In reality the powers of the workers' council are very much restricted by state regulation and by political intervention. The participation of rank-and-file employees in important policy-making areas is almost nil.

(b) Yugoslav workers have not shown any marked desire to participate in management. Many of them are not keen to sit on committees. They do not have the aptitude or the inclination to acquire. The detailed knowledge required for effective participation the desire to participate is not universal. A worker may prefer, for instance, football to participation.

(c) The workers in general do not have any long-term interest in the development of the enterprise. They ceaselessly exert pressure for higher wages, which the management finds difficult to resist. According to Nove, 'there is widespread belief in Yugoslavia that the system as it is today cannot continue'.

■ Employee involvement at the Ford plant in Ohio

This Ford plant employs 3500 workers. By 1980 it was facing a critical situation and it was feared that the factory would be closed down. The quality of production was extremely poor and labour grievances were mounting. Today, as a result of the E.I. programme, the quality has improved by 60 per cent and grievances are reduced to 50 per cent. A 400-page Bible of the employee involvement programme has been prepared.

This programme is run on the following lines:

(1)A committee with an equal number of labour and management representatives is in charge of this programme. It meets twice a month.

(2)The programme consists of two sets of teams who meet on company time every week.

(3)There are 64 production floor teams and 16 white collar teams.
(4)The workers' teams consist of 8-10 workers and a facilitator.
(5)The meetings are informal and they set their own agendas. The duration is about an hour.
(6)This programme is not a substitute for the grievance system and it does not deal with matters falling within the sphere of collective bargaining.

The underlying philosophy is best expressed by Professor Guest, a renowned authority on organisational behaviour, 'there is a gold mine of creativity that can be unleashed at the lower levels.' The programme has sharpened the quality consciousness of the workers. It is estimated that about 2.3 million workers are actively taking part in such projects in the USA.

■ Limits to participation

If participation is to be fruitful, all concerned must be clearly aware of its limitations. The main limitations, briefly, are:

(a)The desire for participation is not universal, nor unlimited. Participation involves additional stress and strain which everyone may not be able to withstand. It is also a matter of choice. The British worker, for instance, prefers a bigger pay packet (and more leisure) to participation. This also partly accounts for the relative backwardness of British industry.

(b) The scope for participation may be restricted by the structure and size of the enterprise and the nature of the task.

(c)The unions may or may not prefer to participate. This is partly a matter of ideology and partly a matter of strategy. A staunch marxist union may have no faith in such devices which Marxists feel are designed to pacify the revolutionary urge of the working class. Some unions may feel that participation leads to confusion of roles and curtails their freedom of action.

(d) Industrial management is now a highly specialised task and trade union representatives cannot be expected to possess the necessary expertise to manage a large enterprise. It is said that workers no more want to manage a firm than to be their own doctors. The John Lewis Partnership (U.K) is owned by the employees themselves but they prefer to leave management in the hands of experts.

(e)Creative decisions are often the result of individual judgement and vision. Group decision-making may be useful for evaluating ideas, but it may inhibit highly original ideas.

(f) Innovative decisions involve serious risk and in a participative framework there is little scope for such decisions.

(g) Participation can lead to inordinate delays. It is difficult to arrive at unanimity when interests clash, the alternatives are many and the perspectives differ.

(h) Participation may dilute responsibility and diffuse accountability. Since no one is exclusively responsible for anything, there is always the danger that decisions may be taken without thorough study.

(i) The participative decision-making process may not be able to match the swiftness of events in this age of discontinuity and uncertainty. The tender plant of participation may grow best in a climate of assured growth and prosperity. It may be easily uprooted in stormy conditions.

To sum up, it may be said that the best results are obtained when the extent of participation is somewhat greater than realistically expected, but still within the capacity of the participants to respond to it effectively. It follows from this, that participation at the shop-floor level would be most satisfying and fruitful. And this has been amply proved by the success of QCs in Japan.

■ Conclusion

Workers' participation in management is being extended in different ways throughout the world. Even the conservative Ford company in America has successfully bunched a novel programme called Employee Involvement. We cannot afford to lag behind.

India happens to be one of the poorest countries in the world with about forty per cent of her population living below the poverty line. Unbridled industrial conflict is not only dehumanising but economically ruinous, particularly for the poor people. The need for constructive participation is imperative.

For participation to succeed, management will have to assume leadership. The old concept of coercive power should be discarded. Power is the capacity to produce intended results and this is done best with co-operation between management and labour, as in Japan. This type of power has been called coactive power by Mary Follett. Coercive power leads to considerable wastage of human talent and effort, while coactive power means co-operative endeavour which ensures the best possible use of human capabilities. In order to inspire confidence, it must move in the direction of an egalitarian society. It should therefore eschew conspicuous consumption. It must show genuine concern for the well-being of workers. And above all, it must be guided by national interest and its practices must be above board.

Similarly, trade unions must realise that what impairs the efficiency of public sector undertakings is harmful not only to the nation but is ultimately harmful to the workers themselves. They have to take a wider and long-term view of their responsibilities and support genuine participation in a constructive manner. The working class as a whole can look forward to a better standard of living, only if productivity improves and economic development is accelerated.

■ Quality circles

In Japan quality circles are called quality control circles. Although a beginning was made in 1949, they were put on a systematic basis in 1962 by the Union of Japanese Scientists and Engineers. The initial inspiration came from Dr. W.E. Deming, a renowned American expert on quality control. QCs have now achieved great success in Japan and the QC movement is spreading throughout the world.

■ Total quality control

The concept of quality control is a familiar one, but the new concept of total quality control is much wider in scope. It implies a company-wide drive for quality improvement in which everyone participates, right from the managing director to the sweeper.

The normal practice is to have a separate quality control department which invariably gives rise to friction between the production departments and the quality control department. The

Japanese practice is to combine the two functions and every worker is equally concerned with both aspects of production, quantity and quality. So exacting are the Japanese quality standards that an American car, for instance, cannot be sold in Japan unless it is repainted in Japan.

The Japanese borrowed the concept of zero-defects from America and transformed it into a vigorous national movement. While zero-defects aimed at achieving specified quality standards, QCs aim at continuous improvement in quality, well beyond the specified standards.

QC programmes are not confined to the quality of the product alone but they aim at a total revolution in the working of the organisation at the shop floor level.

In Japan this movement has achieved astonishing results. There are at present over one hundred thousand registered QCs in Japan, with a total membership of about a million workers. The average QC produces, each year, fifty to sixty implemented suggestions per worker. The current record is held by a company with an average of ninety implemented suggestions per worker for a single year. Nissan Motor Works, with 57,000 persons, has 4,200 QCs and in one year, these circles made 1.12 million suggestions, of which 80% were accepted and suitably rewarded in cash. The firm has nearly doubled its productivity in ten years. QCs have no doubt played a key role in establishing the supremacy of Japanese industry in several fields throughout the world.

■ Main objectives

The Union of Japanese Scientists and Engineers has succinctly stated the main objectives of QCs as follows:

(i) Contribute to the improvement and development of the enterprise.

(ii) Respect humanity and build a happy, bright, workshop which is meaningful to work in.

(iii) Display human capabilities fully and eventually draw out infinite possibilities.

Basic ideas

The basic ideas embodied in the QC can be briefly stated as follows:

(a) There is a natural urge in every human being to achieve excellence in his work. If he is properly guided and encouraged, he can improve his performance endlessly.

(b) The men who are doing a particular job are the real experts as far as that job is concerned. There are many small things that go wrong and they can make valuable suggestions to eliminate such deficiencies and improve the system of production.

(c) Workers are endowed with intelligence and imagination. They possess an intimate knowledge of their jobs and related skills. They aspire for achievement and long for responsible work. If they are treated as human beings, and not as interchangeable parts, there can be an explosion of creativity in the organisation.

(d) The quality circle is not something like a machine, but it is akin to a continuous process. It has two distinct but complementary features. On the one hand it is an educational and learning process. On the other hand, it is a process that facilitates participation of workers in decisions concerning their daily work. This provides a basis for mutual co-operation between management and workers.

The workers are not interchangeable parts.

QCs in Toyota

The following is an account of the working of a quality circle in Toyota, which conveys vividly the Japanese way of conducting QCs.

'M was a team chief and leader of a group of nine workers. He had been leading the group for five years and told his story with the help of an overhead projector and sixty transparencies, many of them in cartoon form. The group was known as the Hottomanzu (Hot Man's) Group. Its basic spirit was to emphasise harmony and co-operation. The four pillars of the house of improvement were co-operation, initiative, harmony, and work satisfaction. They held meetings twice a month, but things did not go very well in the initial period, which he called the "groping disorderly in darkness period". Many did not come to the meetings. There was a tendency for a few to monopolize the discussion. Too much depended on the leader. Too many had the attitude: "Tell me what to do and I'll do it. Let those who are keen be keen if they want; other people can do what they like; I am getting on with my own job".

'M decided that some stimulus was needed. He proposed that they should set themselves the objective of winning a prize for group achievement. There was opposition on the grounds that it was too difficult to be effective because it was not a production department. M convinced them that even in the boiler house, improvements were possible. They actually did get a prize for a project to improve the efficiency of an electric furnace. But there were still too many reluctant passengers, people who thought they were just being too obedient to orders from above. Here M decided that new methods were necessary. He got engineers to come and advise on particular technical problems. At one stage, he declared a three-month moratorium on meetings so that they could start again with fresh enthusiasm. He rated the contributions of his group members under various headings: speaking, reporting back, doing the summary work for reporting, co-operativeness, attendance, contribution to solving problems, etc. He studied the personalities of the members of his group to see how they could be better integrated into a harmonious team, and introduced the habit of shouting "good morning" the first thing on entering the shop in a firm, loud, positive, and enthusiastic voice until even the misanthropes were forced to respond. And so it went on.'

There is no doubt that QCs have been incredibly successful in Japan. Japan's export drive has been so successful that it is compared to a blitz. The success of QCs is basically due to (a) The Japanese work-ethic; (b) Mutual trust between management and workers; and (c) Trade union co-operation.

Japanese firms are run primarily in the interest of employees themselves, who are naturally extremely productivity conscious. There is no denying the fact that the Japanese are most disciplined and diligent in their work. In the famous Toyota factory, they work to the point of utter exhaustion, to the limits of human endurance. They are often indignant. They curse their firm and fate. And yet they work with untiring energy. They are unbelievably time-conscious. A foreman once told his workers: 'Here, at this position we have five unused seconds'. If the foreman is absent, they would work harder to make up for him. Toyota workers made in one year 200,000 suggestions for improving productivity, as against only 25 official grievances. A comparable American firm registered 12,000 grievances from its 11,000 workers during this period.

■ Quality circle movement in India

QCs were first launched in the Hyderabad Unit of BHEL in 1980. There are now about 1400 QCs in the various branches of BHEL throughout India. The response has been encouraging.

The Quality Circle Forum of India was formed in 1982 and the movement is progressing. Some private firms have also launched QCs successfully.

■ Dr. Deming's advice to top management and quality circles

Deming has become a most respected guru for the Japanese. When in 1950 he was first invited to Japan to lecture on statistical quality control, he introduced a wide range of simple analytical techniques. The Japanese were fascinated by the 'Deming Wheel', which refers to Deming's Plan-Do-Check-Act cycle of operations. In recognition of his contribution to the field of quality control, the Japanese established the prestigious Deming Prize, the very next year.

Although an American expert has been responsible for the revolutionary innovation of QCs, these circles have not been very successful in America so far. In point of fact, in the famous Silicon Valley described as the Mecca of twenty-first century management, QCs have been almost a dismal failure. It is said that the average worker would not attend his next quality circle meeting if it was the last day on earth. According to Deming, American management is primarily responsible for this failure.

In his provocative address to students of management at Utah University, Deming was forthright in his criticism of management.

'People all over the world think that it is the factory worker that causes problems. He is not your problem. Ever since there has been anything such as industry, the factory worker has known that quality is what will protect his job. He knows that poor quality in the hands of the customer will lose the market and will cost him his job. He is not allowed to do it because the management wants figures, more products, and never mind the quality. They measure only in figures. The factory worker is forced to make defective products, forced to turn out defective items.... He is totally helpless. If he tries to do something about it, he might as well talk to the wall. Nobody listens.'

Earlier, in the same speech he told the students that 'the most important figures are those that are unknown or unknowable'. A very bold statement for a statistician to make.

Deming is extremely critical of American management which, he says, has on the whole a negative value. 'It is like an old refrigerator you cannot sell.' According to him, 85 per cent of the waste is due to the failure of the system and only 15 per cent due to local faults. Management is therefore mostly to be blamed for law productivity and inferior quality. Deming has therefore formulated a list of 14 top management obligations which deserve most careful consideration. These principles are not sufficiently known in India. The following are the most important of these principles.

Deming's principles: Obligations of top management

1. Innovate and allocate resources to fulfil the long-range needs of the company and customer, rather than short-term profitability.
2. Reduce the number of multiple-source suppliers. Price has no meaning without an integral consideration for quality. Encourage suppliers to use statistical process control
3. Institute more thorough and better job-related training.
4. Reduce fear throughout the organisation by encouraging open, two-way, nonpunitive communication. The economic loss resulting from fear of asking questions or reporting trouble is appalling.
5. Help reduce waste by encouraging design, research, and sales people to learn more about the problems of production.
6. Eliminate the use of goals and slogans to encourage productivity, unless training and management support is also provided.
7. Closely examine the impact of work standards. Do they consider quality or help anyone do a better job? They often act as an impediment to productivity improvement.

This is a very perceptive and daring piece of advice. Deming has no faith in industrial engineering techniques such as work measurement. Simply stated, it means eliminate work standards that prescribe numerical quotas. Deming is known for his audacious thinking and the Americans are prepared to pay his fabulous seminar fees ($ 20,000!), but they seem to ignore his advice!

8. Institute a vigorous programme for training people in new skills, to keep up with changes in materials, methods, product design, and machinery.

The remaining principles relate mostly to statistical training and the use of statistical techniques.

Institute job-related training

The Pontiac *Fiero* which was the first American car produced from scratch, strictly according to Deming's advice, has broken all US sales records for a two-seater car. Pontiac chose a single supplier for each item for this car, without competitive bidding

There is one point which is missing from Deming's fourteen principles referred to above. It is that Japanese firms take utmost pains to cultivate, sustain, and develop a healthy work ethic in their organisations. Training in Japan, which is lifetime training, is not only technical and management-oriented, but it is also ethical. The induction training programmes in large Japanese firms are most carefully planned, as explained in the next chapter.

The quality circle movement is still in its infancy in India and it is essential for management to bear in mind Deming's valuable advice. There is no better authority on the subject of QCs.

To conclude briefly (a) As Deming has pointed out, the success of QCs depends largely on management philosophy and practice. (b) In the Indian situation the need for ethical training is of paramount importance as the Indian work ethic is being rapidly eroded.

■ The quality of working life: A new concept

In 1972 an unusual strike occurred at the General Motors assembly plant at Lordstown, Ohio. This strike was in protest against meaningless work and authoritarian management. In other words, this strike was not for higher wages, but for a better quality of working life.

It is not possible to define the quality of working life precisely. By its very nature, quality does not lend itself to easy quantification. For instance, beauty cannot be measured. But it is possible to give some broad indications of the various aspects of the quality of working life. These aspects are briefly discussed below.

■ Adequate wages, salaries

Employees should receive an adequate salary so that they can maintain themselves properly. The salaries must also be fair and equitable. They should be comparable with salaries for similar jobs in comparable firms. Salaries also need to be related to the cost of living and other considerations.

■ Sale and healthy environment

Work should not involve any unnecessary hazards. Workers should not be exposed to unhealthy conditions -- overcrowding, poisonous fumes, and badly polluted air. Steps will have to be taken to reduce odours, noise, heat, and such other annoyances. This is the negative aspect. The positive aspect is that factories should be designed well and the work place should look cheerful and invigorating.

■ Development of human talent

Work should afford full scope for the flowering of human talent. This is the most compelling human need. A man fulfils himself only when he develops his abilities to the maximum possible extent. In the modern world such development must generally take place through employment work. Meaningful, interesting, and challenging work is perhaps the most important aspect of the quality of working life.

Advancement

This has three aspects. In the first place, work should afford scope for the use and development of the knowledge and skills of an employee. If an electrical engineer is assigned a job which does not require any knowledge of electrical engineering, this is wasteful. The employee's knowledge will rust. Again, when an employee acquires some new knowledge and experience, his future work assignments should make proper use of this new knowledge and experience. Advancement has a social purpose too. It is a recognition of the employee's work achievements. Friends and family's love, affection, and respect are enhanced by advancement. Promotion to a position of great responsibility is the most visible proof of anyone's success in working life.

The total life space

The concept of total life space needs some explanation. Work is no doubt the central part of a man's life. But there are also other aspects to it. For instance, the individual has a responsibility towards his family. He must educate his children well. If, on promotion, he is transferred to a place where there are no proper schools, his children will suffer. His family life may be disrupted by frequent tours, transfers, and continuous night-shifts. Work which is so demanding as to deprive an individual of his leisure is also harmful. In sum, the concept of the total life space means a life in which various requirements such as the individual's health, happiness and development, as well as the requirements of organisational work, are properly balanced.

Social relevance

An organisation which does not care for the well-being of the community and recklessly destroys natural resources and aggravates pollution cannot win social recognition and respect. Similarly, if an organisation indulges in unethical practices, it will invite serious criticism. People who have a sense of value may not like to work in such organisations.

Complex issues

It is obvious that the concept of the quality of working life is complex. Many intangibles are involved and perfect arrangements are not conceivable. At the same time, there are some areas where positive action is possible. For instance, work can be organised so as to provide fuller scope for human endowments.

■ Work in America

This is the title of a special report prepared by experts for the United States Government. The report aroused a good deal of interest and controversy. The report highlights the adverse effects of the present-day methods of work organisation. It points out that employees have become indifferent to the quality of work. Work is disrupted as a result of higher turnover, absenteeism, sudden stoppages of work, and even sabotage of plant and machinery. It also affects the health and family life of workers. Society suffers in the process. There is a general revulsion against work in industry. Some critics do not subscribe to these views. They feel that only a small minority is affected in this manner. Further, there is not really much scope for changing the present pattern of work and organisation. Mostly people expect only good salaries and take nothing else seriously. According to this school of thought, money is more important that the quality of working life.

■ Novel reorganisation of factories

■ The whole man goes to work

Industrial organisations, as they are organised today, stunt the growth of the individual, whose vision is impaired, and who is maimed and crippled. They are like prisons which suffocate the spirit of man. His vital human attributes such as imagination, capacity to think, his emotions, aspirations, and values, are totally ignored. The whole man with these attributes goes to work, where he is treated as only having a pair of hands.

The problems of employee dissatisfaction with the present pattern of organisations cannot be tackled easily. Industrial organisations need to be designed in a radically different way, befitting the dignity of man.

Work should be so organised that it gives the workers a sense of fulfilment and provides an opportunity for psychological growth which has many dimensions, such as:

Capacity to operate more and more complex machines and processes;

Capacity to analyse data;

Capacity for innovation in different fields--technical, management, industrial relations, etc.

Capacity to influence people, to lead people;

Capacity to teach and educate;

Capacity to make difficult decisions; and

Capacity for research and development.

Two such cases of radical reorganisation of factories are briefly described below:

Reorganisation of a thread factory

In this thread shop, work is fully automated. There is one worker at the point where the thread comes out of the automated line. The shop was organised in order to achieve the following results:

(a) Highest possible proportion of top grade thread;

(b) Minimisation of rejects; and

(c) Lowest possible cost of production per tonne of good grade thread.

It was decided to reorganise the factory with the following objectives in view:

(a) To develop a flexible organisation which would facilitate further innovations;

(b)To minimise physical and psychological strain resulting from automatic work. In other words, to make the work more interesting by providing scope for initiative.

The nature of reorganisation

Briefly, the reorganisation involved the following steps. The plant was subdivided into semi-autonomous groups. One special feature of the reorganisation was the limitation of the charge hand. His work was to be done by the group or the foreman himself.

Reorganisation

The annual targets were fixed by the departmental head, while planning was done by him every month or every week in consultation with the foreman.

The group itself managed its day-to-day work such as allocation of work to individuals, watching the progress of work, and inspection.

The management, however, reserved to itself the power to appoint the foreman and to recruit new workers.

Maximum possible delegation was the guiding principle in this reorganisation. When a group is given definite responsibilities and the freedom to meet them, it functions at its best.

The results were encouraging. Absenteeism declined over a period of two years. The production of top grade thread went up and the cost of production was also reduced.

■ A new pet-food factory

As discussed earlier, workers are now well-educated and they naturally aspire for a better quality of working life. They want work that will be challenging and afford scope for personal development. They want opportunities for thinking, imagining, decision-making, and creating something new. They want egalitarian treatment which enhances self-respect. Simply stated, day-to-day work should be meaningful, befitting the dignity of man. Richard E. Walton, a noted social scientist, established a new pet-food factory to meet these requirements.

Autonomous work groups

The entire workforce of 70 employees was divided into six teams, each consisting of 7-14 persons under a team leader. In each shift there was a processing team and a packaging team.

Allocation of work

The packaging team was responsible for loading and storage of materials, drawing the ingredients from the stores, mixing them and transforming them into the finished product, involving a series of operations.

The packing team looked after packaging of finished goods, warehousing and shipping.

Freedom to plan daily work

The teams organised their daily work in a manner they thought best. They handled manufacturing problems that arose from time to time. They redistributed work, if necessary, if some of the employees were absent on a particular day.

Team responsibilities

The teams were responsible for plant maintenance, quality control, industrial engineering, and personnel matters. Each member had to maintain his plant and machinery and each team carried out quality tests for the product. This constituted self-management, covering all aspects of production.

Design of jobs

In designing the jobs, it was ensured that every job involved the exercise of human abilities of a higher order, such as planning, thinking, analysing, and securing the co-operation of others. For this reason, the truck lift operator was given the additional work of warehouse planning and shipping activities. Every job was thus made meaningful as it provided opportunities for using one's talent, knowledge, and imagination. It was naturally challenging and interesting. The feeling of alienation was thus greatly reduced. One developed an affinity for one's job in this atmosphere.

All jobs on a par

The jobs were so structured that they were all on a par in terms of the skills needed and responsibilities involved. There was therefore only one category of workers. Financial incentives were, however, provided for mastering new tasks first in the team and later in the whole organisation.

Results

These can be briefly summarised as follows:

(a) While industrial engineers had estimated the manpower requirements at 110, the plant was managed with only 70 persons.

(b) Annual savings to the extent of $ 600,000 were achieved as a result of reduction in fixed overheads and variable manufacturing costs. Absenteeism was restricted and rejections were reduced by 92%. This was a clear indication that the employees did their work thoroughly.

(c) The reactions of the workers were particularly encouraging:

'I never get bored.... I can make my own decisions.' They enjoyed their work much better.

Conclusion

This was an innovative exercise in setting up a new factory. The approach was superior to the job enrichment approach, where each job was considered in isolation. The industrial engineering approach is mechanical and while perhaps it may be economical

Ensure that the employee is suited to the job

in the short run, its long-term consequences may prove to be harmful. The basic consideration is to ensure that every employee has a job best suited to his knowledge, talent and aptitude.

CHAPTER 4

Education for good work

The job is the centre of life

Most people work in order to live, but very few master the art of working. Work is not a part of life, but life itself. Even in affluent countries like the USA where adequate unemployment benefits are provided, the unemployed person is unhappy and miserable. He loses his dignity, self-respect, and self-confidence. He becomes morose, depressed, and melancholy. He also loses self-control and becomes addicted to vices such as gambling, drugs, and liquor. His family also suffers equally. Many people eagerly look forward to the bliss of retirement, but die soon afterwards because they find themselves in a void. They are the victims of boredom and brooding.

Research conducted by Dr. Harvey Brenner of Johns Hopkins University, USA, has shown that as the unemployment rate rises, so does the number of heart attacks and admissions to mental hospitals. These findings are also supported by research carried out in other countries.

Paradoxically enough, people who have spent a long, anxious time searching for a job, start neglecting their work no sooner than they are employed. They are not aware of the harm they are doing to themselves, their organisation, as well as their community. They are, in fact, undermining the very foundation of the organisation which provides them with work. It is like destroying the foundation of one's own house.

On the other hand, organisations utilise only a very small fraction of the human potential at their disposal. This is lamentable from every point of view. Organisation work provides very little scope for man's knowledge, his talent, his urge for creativity and co-operation. How this can be done is discussed in Chapter 3.

Unemployment breeds addiction

The theme of this chapter is: Education for Good Work. The individual who does not understand the vital importance of work does great harm to himself and his community unknowingly. Education for good work is badly neglected in India. As long back as in 1895, Lokamanya Tilak castigated the Indian people for their extreme laziness. Similarly Mahatma Gandhi told Colin Clark, an eminent economist, that 'the source of India's trouble was that the people were thoroughly idle'. But there have not been any systematic efforts for educating people for good work.

■ Aims of education for good work

The aims may be briefly stated as follows:

To enable the individual to understand various aspects of work, such as psychological, social, moral, economic, and aesthetic.

And thus to enable him to realise that there is no joy of life, without joy of work. He can perceive the grandeur of life only through his work.

It is rightly said that every individual is a special kind of artist, who can shape his personality through his work. He can beautify his own life and that of his community through his work. Such a man can die happily, saying to himself that he has worked all along to the best of his ability, and thus fulfilled himself. His good work survives even after his death.

■ Human life minus work is equal to zero

This proposition is based on the following considerations.

■ Work banishes the three great evils—boredom, vice, and poverty.

This is the profound conclusion which Voltair reaches in his classic novel *Candide.*

Voltaire was a phenomenon. He is reckoned to be one of the wittiest writers of all times and *Candide* is his wittiest novel. It is also a profoundly philosophical novel. It deals with the question why there is so much evil in human life. The story in outline is as follows:

Voltaire's masterpiece — Candide

Candide is a young lad of extremely agreeable and sweet disposition, living as a dependant with a Baron in Westphalia. He is deeply in love with the Baron's daughter, Cunegonde, 'a buxom girl of seventeen, with a fresh, rosy complexion, altogether seductive'. One day as they were leaving the dinner table, Candide picked up the handkerchief dropped by Cunegonde. Thereupon 'she quite innocently took his hand, he as innocently kissed her with singular grace and ardour. Their lips met, their eyes flashed, their knees trembled....' But all this was noticed by the Baron, who naturally became extremely furious. He expelled Candide from the house at once 'with powerful kicks on the backside'. Cunegonde was also severely boxed on the ears by her mother for this gross misbehaviour. *Candide* is a moving account of the grotesque and ghastly experiences which befall the lot of its hero.

Cunegonde is equally unfortunate. Soon after Candide is expelled, one night, while she is asleep, bulgars invade their mansion and slaughter her parents. A six-foot tall Bulgar sets about ravishing her which she resists with all her might. The brute wounds her left thigh. She is, however, rescued by a gallant Bulgar captain with whom she has to live for some time as his mistress, washing his shirts and cooking his meals. At the end of three months, he gets tired of her. He has also no money left and sells her to a Jew who has a weakness for women. The Jew in turn is forced to share her beauty with the Grand Inquisitor. According to the agreement Cunegonde belongs to the Jew on Monday, Wednesday and Sabbath days, and to the Inquisitor the other days of the week. There is some quarrelling as to whom Cunegonde belongs on Saturday night. Such are the bizarre happenings in this story.

There are two other interesting characters, Pangloss and Martin. Both are philosophers. Pangloss is the family tutor, an ardent follower of Leibnitz, the great German philosopher. He maintains that we live in the best of all possible worlds, where everything is connected and arranged for the best. Martin, on the other hand, is an arch realist. He holds the view that man was created by the forces of evil and not by the forces of good. 'I am forced to believe that man's origin is evil.'

After a seemingly unending succession of disasters and catastrophies, Candide and Cunegonde are united and Candide decides to settle on a small farm near Constantinople along with his two friends, Pangloss and Martin. At heart Candide is sad and disillusioned. Cunegonde has lost all her beauty. She has grown ugly, and has become cantankerous and insufferable. Candide has no longer the desire to marry her but does so merely because of her persistence.

Candide is constantly perplexed by the question: Why is there so much suffering, so much evil in human life? Why are men so mean, so oppressive, so cruel and brutal? Can man ever be happy and civilized? One day when the boredom becomes intolerable, they decide to consult a

'Man's origin is evil'

great philosopher living in the neighbourhood. However he provides no useful guidance.

At this time, while the conversation is in progress, news comes that two cabinet ministers and a judge are strangled in Constantinople. As they are proceeding to their little farm, they see an old farmer sitting at his door under an arbour of orange trees, enjoying fresh air. He looks perfectly healthy, vigorous and cheerful. Pangloss asks him the name of the judge who is strangled. He says that he has no idea and he never bothers about what happens in Constantinople. 'I send my garden stuff to be sold there, and that is enough for me.'

The farmer then invites them—Candide, Pangloss and Martin—into his house, where they are offered exquisite refreshments such as they had never seen before. After the refreshments their beards are perfumed by the farmer's two daughters.

Thereafter takes place the following dialogue:

'You must have a magnificent estate,' said Candide to the Turk.

'Only twenty acres replied the Turk, 'my children help me to farm it, and we find that the work banishes those three great evils—boredom, vice, and poverty.'

As he walked back to the farm, Candide reflected on what the Turk had said. 'That old fellow', said he, turning to Pangloss and Martin, 'seemed to me to have done much better for himself than six kings'.

'High estate', said Pangloss, 'is always dangerous, as every philosopher knows.'

'I also know', said Candide, 'that we must go and work in the garden.'

'You are quite right', said Pangloss. 'When man was placed in the Garden of Eden, he was put there "to dress it and to keep it", to work in fact; which proves that man was not born to an easy life.'

'We must work without arguing', said Martin. 'That is the only way to make life bearable.'

Martin's wise words deserve to be written on the tablets of our hearts. Martin is a practical man who sees the futility of abstract metaphysical discussions.

■ Work is as essential as food, water, and air

The human body generates a certain amount of mental and physical energy for which work is the best outlet. As a noted author has said, "You ask why I go on working. I go on working for the same reason that a hen goes on laying eggs." Without work, man suffocates. He needs it as much as he needs air. Work keeps a man healthy and vigorous. It enriches his personality in several ways.

The case of the celebrated musician, Pablo Casals, illustrates in a striking manner how even at a very advanced age work can have a rejuvenating influence on the human body and mind.

The miraculous case of Pablo Casals

When Pablo Casals had reached the age of ninety, he was a physical wreck, suffering from arthritis and breathing difficulties. He could walk only with the greatest difficulty. His hands were swollen and fingers clenched.

His daily routine was interesting. His lovely young wife would help him start the day at 8 a.m. Before breakfast, he would go to the piano. As he started playing the piano, his physical disabilities gradually disappeared. The fingers slowly unlocked, his back straightened and he could breathe freely. This was nothing short of a miracle.

'He hummed as he played, and said that Bach spoke to him there.... His entire body seemed fused with the music.' After completing his musical piece, he would go to the breakfast table, eat heartily and talk animatedly. And then he would go for a walk on the beach.

After an hour or so he would come back and then work on his correspondence until lunch, and then take a nap. Afterwards the clenched hands and other physical disabilities would reappear!

■ Without strenuous work, there is no genuine leisure

People long for leisure, for holidays. But more often than not they are simply bored on holidays. A glass of icecold water is very satisfying only when one is thirsty. Similarly a holiday can be truly enjoyable only if one is exhausted by work

There are some advocates of abundant leisure. They argue that man can be truly happy, humane, and creative only when he is freed from the drudgery of work. But this is a delusion. Excessive leisure makes life futile, rather than satisfying.

And if everyone thinks that his day-to-day work is best avoided or is to be done without any commitment, our economic and social life will soon be disorganised. Enjoyment of leisure is possible only if all the amenities the modern world has to offer are readily available. If, for instance, the milkman does not turn up in the morning, the trains do not run on schedule, and drinking water is not available, how can anyone enjoy his leisure?

The relationship between work and leisure is interesting. The more exacting the work, the more enjoyable is the leisure that follows. For example, in his young days, Bertrand Russell used to go on long walking tours during holidays. He would walk as much as forty miles a day. At the end of the day, he says, it was

Holidays can be enjoyable only after exhaustive work

the greatest pleasure merely to sit down and relax. Nothing else was needed.

Wittgenstein, a great philosopher, used to be absolutely exhausted by his lectures. Immediately after a lecture was over he would rush off to a cinema, buying a bun or cake, and munch it while watching the film from the very first row of seats. He would be totally absorbed in the film even if it was quite trivial and boring. He used to say: 'This is like a shower bath!'

■ Leisure enriches work

Leisure enriches our work in several ways. First it dispels fatigue and enables the individual to view his problems afresh in a relaxed frame of mind. If an executive makes decisions when he is tired, depressed, and exhausted, he is likely to reach wrong decisions. A simple problem may appear very difficult to him. He may lose his temper, and become impatient and hasty. A wise administrator makes important decisions only when he is fresh.

Secondly, when one is resting, the unconscious mind may continue to work on an unresolved problem. It may suggest new ideas. Important discoveries are made in this manner.

David Ogilvy, the advertising wizard, once dreamed about an old baker driving his horse and wagon along a country lane on his way to deliver bread. An advertisement based on this dream proved to be popular for the next twenty-five years!

Work can easily be spoiled, and wrong decisions taken if one is overworked and exhausted. Russell had perfected the art of using his leisure wisely and creatively. He had realised that all good work requires a period of subconscious incubation so that the ideas germinate underground and the solutions then emerge with blinding clarity. This is how he describes the process in *Portraits from Memory*.

How a holiday revived Russell's flagging energy

'I had undertaken to give the Lowell Lectures at Boston, and had chosen as my subject "Our Knowledge of the External World". Throughout 1913 I thought about this topic. In term time in my rooms at Cambridge, in vacations in a quiet inn on the upper reaches of the Thames, I concentrated with such intensity that I sometimes forgot to breathe and emerged panting as from a trance. But all to no avail. To every theory that I could think of, I could perceive fatal objections. At last, in despair, I went off to Rome for Christmas, hoping that a holiday would revive my flagging energy. I got back to Cambridge on the last day of 1913, and although my difficulties were still completely unresolved I arranged, because the remaining time was short, to dictate as best I could to a stenographer. Next morning, as she came in at the door, I suddenly saw exactly what I had to say, and proceeded to dictate the whole book without a moment's hesitation.'

■ Work can give us aesthetic delight

Everybody yearns for fresh aesthetic experiences. Such experiences are exhilarating. They energise us.

To produce something beautiful is a matter of lasting happiness. Artists are absorbed in their creative work. But it need not be supposed that such happiness is possible only for the artists. Even small routine things can be done beautifully. Office letters can be typed neatly and accurately. In anything that one does there is always scope for order, proportion, and symmetry.

■ Work can satisfy the innate human urge for dignity and self-respect

Man is perennially in quest of dignity and self-respect. He values self-respect above everything else. He prefers to work in an organisation where he can play an important role.

A twenty-two year old women, who was earlier working in a firm of architects accepted the job as secretary in a surgery on a lower salary. She loved the job although the working conditions

Everybody must feel that his job is important

were poor, because she said, 'I wanted to meet people'. 'I feel I am doing a necessary job.'

'One morning a woman of thirty with six children comes in... she greets me cheerfully and thanks me for the help I have been able to give her; this is the most rewarding part of my job'.

In a good organisation everybody must feel that his work is important. This is the art of management.

■ Men may work for different reasons but together they shape life and society

Consider the following well-known story of three stone cutters.

Three stone-cutters were building a temple. They were asked by a passerby what they were doing. 'I am a poor man. I have to maintain my family. I am making a living here', said the first stone-cutter. 'Well, I work because I want to show that I am the best stone-cutter in the country,' said the second one with an air of pride. 'Oh! I want to build the most beautiful temple in the country', said the third one, with a visionary gleam in his eyes.

Their jobs are identical, but their perspectives are vastly different and yet together they can build a magnificent temple.

■ Participative work provides an opportunity for self-expression and self-development

Factory or office work is often so minutely subdivided that it becomes totally meaningless. It does not provide any outlet for the deeper layers of personality. The worker becomes alienated, morose, and develops a feeling of nothingness. On the other hand, if workers are encouraged to participate in the decision-making process related to their work, they develop a sense of belonging to the organisation. Participation provides opportunities for self-expression and self-development. The Quality Circle movement is based on this principle. It has led to the explosion of creativity in Japanese organisations.

■ Work can be play

When an individual identifies himself completely with his work, it becomes as interesting and pleasing as play itself. Robert Frost in a little poem called *Two Tramps in Mud Time* has expressed this idea beautifully It is the beginning of spring. Trees are without leaves. Snow is turning into mud. Frost is out in the garden splitting wood, for the first time after winter, which he greatly enjoys. Two tramps are watching him regretfully, because they feel that they are deprived of their work and bread. This creates a dilemma for Frost, because he does not want to give up the work which he loves so dearly. Frost concludes:

> My object in living is to unite
> My avocation and my vacation
> As my two eyes are one in sight.

Day-to-day work can be a playful activity. One of David Ogilvy's maxims of good management is: 'Make it *fun* to work in your agency'.

■ Work can be creative

'Some people see things that are and ask why: I dream of things that never were and ask why not'—Bernard Shaw

Man is supremely happy when he succeeds in creating something that is altogether new, useful, or beautiful. It is not that only scientists, technologists, and artists can create. Creativity is possible in all fields and at all levels. Even a primary school teacher can be creative. An uneducated American dirt farmer, George Krug, made a great contribution to the development of hybrid corn many years ago.

Robert E. Wood, a young American executive, wrote a long memorandum in which he advocated a change-over from the prevailing mail order business to the establishment of retail chain stores. This brought about a great marketing revolution in America.

Creativity grows in the soil of grinding work. For instance, Edison worked for five days and nights during the development of his phonograph. He took no more than four or five hours sleep while working on this invention. Burnel, probably the most innovative and daring Victorian engineer, directed the work of the *Great Eastern* from his sick-bed. She was his dreamship designed to be six times bigger than any ship afloat at that time. He was at that time also paralysed by a stroke.

■ Economic development depends upon disciplined performance of work

Even if a country is endowed with abundant natural resources like petroleum, without the systematic working of oil refineries it cannot be rich and prosperous. Ultimately man is the creator of all wealth.

It must be noted that work means both manual, and intellectual or knowledge work. Productivity in the modern world depends more upon knowledge and its application than on purely manual work. An aeroplane, which is the product of human knowledge, is several thousand times more productive than the bullock cart.

The Japanese economic miracle is mostly attributed to the Japanese work ethic. On return from a visit to Japan, the Malaysian Prime Minister rightly said, 'Brilliance is buying Japanese, genius is importing the Japanese work ethic itself'.

Japan in the Passing Lane by Kamata is a highly critical account of the Toyota factory management. He refers to a group discussion wherein the team chief says, 'Here, at this position, we have five unused seconds.' Something difficult to believe. Economic development is an exacting task. It cannot be achieved in an easygoing fashion as we seem to believe.

It is this attitude towards work that has enabled Toyota to perfect the famous Just-in-time production system.

■ Work is a moral obligation

People are seldom aware that their comfortable living depends upon the work of several thousands of people. The first thing, for instance, almost every one looks forward to in the morning is a hot cup of tea. This cup of tea embodies the work of many thousand people.

As E.F. Schumacher, in his thought-provoking book *Small Is Beautiful* points out, the educated people have a special obligation to serve their community. He refers to the computations made by the Chinese which show that in order to support one student for a five-year degree course at a university, thirty farmers have to work for five years. The cost of training a graduate is thus equivalent to 150 peasant-work-years. Every educated person must be aware of his obligation to the

Is education passport to privileges?

community and work for its welfare on completion of his education. Schumacher raises the basic question whether education is 'a passport to privilege' or 'a sacred obligation to serve the community'. For an educated person to think constantly in terms of one's privileges is unbecoming. It really amounts to ingratitude. It is exploitation of the very people who have borne the cost of one's education.

A truly educated person must first think of his obligations and responsibilities rather than his rights and privileges.

■ Work is our greatest guru

Work is our lifelong companion as well as our greatest teacher. There are many things which cannot be taught. They can only be learnt. Many skills like swimming, cycling etc., are best acquired by practice only. 'Practice makes a man perfect' is a well-known saying. A good musician, for instance, never misses his daily practice.

Work alone can teach us how to organise the work itself properly. It is an art to know when to work and when to stop work.

In the field of management only the person who assumes responsibility can learn to make proper dicisions. Managerial competence is largely created on the job.

An executive learns best when he is saddled with responsibility, that is, when he is working. It is easy to propose elegant simplistic solutions to complex problems in the class-room or in seminars, but in practice even simple problems may prove insoluble.

To sum up, it can be truly said that work is our greatest teacher, stern as well as benevolent. This guru is silent, yet eloquent and effective. He illuminates, guides, and assists. He is constantly watching us and testing our abilities, aptitudes, devotion, and perseverance. He teaches us many precious things that are often intangible and therefore unteachable. We must always respect him.

■ Work is the real antidote to grief

Grief is part of human life. It is unavoidable as long as death is unavoidable. But it is not wise to allow oneself to sink in grief on the death of a beloved person. One must preserve one's sanity even in times of acute distress. Work alone comes to the rescue of man in such times by providing healthy consolation. The satisfaction that comes from constructive work is the only antidote to grief. In some cases grief itself provides indirectly the inspiration for some noble work. Such at least appears to be the case of Sir James Thomason (1804-53), who is described as the prince of Indian civilians. His young wife died prematurely, a loss which he could hardly bear. Thereafter he bestowed all the care and affection he was capable of on the people he served. His achievements constitute a fine memorial to his beloved wife.

■ It is only through work that man can develop himself fully

Psychologists call it self-actualisation. This is man's most important need. A fully developed person is devoted to his work in the priestly sense—in the sense that work is worship. He takes on responsibility. He thinks independently. He has a sense of values. He tries to understand himself and allows the self to emerge. He is honest to himself and others in all his dealings. He is spontaneous in his behaviour, which is marked by simplicity and naturalness. He is full of joy because he is not inwardly oppressed by mean and low thoughts. He enjoys the intense effort essential to self-actualisation, because every advance in that direction is a moment of genuine happiness. His work then becomes to him the most sacred thing on earth. Work then becomes play to him and he looks upon work as its own reward.

Visvesvaraya was a self-actualiser who had a passion for perfection. As he would say, 'If your business is only to sweep a crossing, remember that it is your duty to make it the best-swept in the world.' To him all work was sacred.

■ It is work that distinguishes man from animals

Two noted psychologists, W.N. and L.A. Kellogg, nurtured a baby chimpanzee along with their own child, with equal care and affection. They wanted to find out whether the chimpanzee would develop like a human being. It was found that the child was developing both physically and psychologically. The child was gaining in weight and height and soon began to crawl and walk. This was physiological growth. But it also started uttering words and sentences. This was psychological growth. The baby chimpanzee on the other hand was developing only physiologically, gaining in weight and height, etc. It did not grow psychologically. It could neither utter words nor could it talk like the child.

Thus, man has two dimensions of growth, physiological and psychological, while animals have only one dimension of growth, physiological.

Psychological growth has many dimensions. Man can acquire new knowledge, he can think, he can develop new ideas. He can be creative and he can be mature and wise. And this is something obvious. The achievements of man in science, technology, and the arts are awe-inspiring. But animals have no such achievements to their credit.

Psychological growth then, differentiates man from animals. And it takes place only through work. Animals do no comparable work. In the final analysis then, it is work that distinguishes man from animals.

Man can think

The consequences that flow from this conclusion are momentous. If a person stops doing any work, his psychological growth is not only stunted, but he also starts degenerating psychologically, losing his capacity to think and capacity to understand. Ultimately, in the worst case, he will not be different from an animal which has zero psychological growth. For a man, psychological growth can even be negative, when he becomes prematurely senile.

It will follow from this that the individual should take as much care of his work as he takes of his health, in his own interest. To shun work is to invite self-destruction.

To sum up, human life is meaningless without work. It becomes an unbearable burden.

■ Manual work is equally important

There is a tendency to look down upon manual work, which is harmful. As John Holt, a great education expert, points out, we can learn much from even the most seemingly unskilled work. He is right when he says that manual work brings us in contact with some part of reality. 'It is in our nature to want to shape the world around us, to make things and do things, and to want to do them as well as we can.' The importance of manual work is clearly recognised in Zen Buddhism. Manual work is an essential element in the life of the Zen monk. For a Zen monk, a day of no manual work is a day of no food. Japanese culture is profoundly influenced by the concept that all work is sacred. Washing a bowl is as important as meditation itself. Purely manual tasks have been made into fine arts. The tea ceremony is a beautiful illustration of this approach. After retirement, Japanese executives gladly accept even simple manual jobs. A retired chief accountant looks after the parking of cars and cleaning a parking plot. He does this work to keep his mind working. He needs no money. A sales manager cleans the ashtrays in the local subway stations. He does this for his health. There are over 200 Silver Talent Centres in Japan which find work for retired persons.

■ Humour always enlivens work in offices and factories

Douglas McGregor's book, *The Human Side of Enterprise,* has become a classic. A book on the humorous side of management should also be likewise a classic. As Sir William Osler, the legendary physician, has said, 'Laughter is the music of life'. People spend the bulk of their time in offices and factories and the dull routine is enlivened by humorous episodes and witty observations. The world of work is inhabitated by persons in all shapes and sizes and all sorts of idiosyncracies mark the scene.

Only a few instances can be quoted here. When Eisenhower was president of Columbia University, the university had engaged a consulting firm to suggest measures for administrative reforms. The consultants recommended that the president's span of control of one hundred and thirty two items should be reduced to three only. Eisenhower rejected the recommendation. The consultants report, which cost $ 80,000, remained the most expensive and least read book the university ever acquired.

Hary Bennett, the right-hand man of Henry Ford, was a most colourful character. He kept lions and tigers as pets. Occasionally he would bring them to work, walking them around Ford's magnificent Rouge Plant on leashes. Sometimes he would slip a lion or a tiger into the back seat of a visitor's car as a joke. Once a lion placed his paw affectionately on the driver's shoulder while the car was going through the city streets. The driver abandoned the car in fear and the lion also got out of the car. This caused great panic and confusion in the street and the police had to shoot the lion.

Eccentric administrators

British officers working in India were seriously handicapped in several ways. They were not accustomed to the tropical, hot, and sometimes humid climate. Their families would be often away in England and the social and cultural atmosphere in India was suffocating for them. Many of them could not adjust to these uncongenial circumstances. And as a result they would become depressed, morose and temperamental. Many of them developed a distaste for work and some acquired queer habits. A few typical examples of eccentric officers are mentioned below.

Some Eccentric Administrators

1. Sandys: District magistrate working on a tree

Sandys was a district magistrate of Bhagalpur (Bihar) who used to dispose of his cases while working on a branch of a tree. All others, lawyers, government servants and members of the public, had to sit on the ground. He felt more comfortable on the branch of a tree than in the dingy courtroom full of dust and cobwebs. He preferred fresh air to artificial ventilation provided by a pankha of dry grass manually operated. He also liked to be away from the crowd. In those days modern amenities like electric fans, air coolers, let alone airconditioners, were non-existent. The maidan where Sandys used to work is still known as 'Sandys' Compound'in Bhagalpur.

2. Forest: Collector of Shahabad district

He was another queer official. He explained the significance of his name as For Rest. He lived in a very spacious bungalow with a huge compound of over 20 acres. He put up four different tents, one for each of the subdivisions under his control, where all papers pertaining to the division were kept. He would work in these tents

Magistrate working on a tree

from time to time. But his instructions to the staff were that they should tell others that he was visiting the particular subdivision (although he was in fact working in the tent for the particular subdivision). These instructions were strictly enforced.

3. Manwaring: Collector of Monghyr district

He was an aristocrat who lived all by himself with access to a well-appointed cellar. Once when after a sumptuous dinner he retired to his bed, he hated to get up to switch off the lights and instead fired his pistol to smash the electric bulb!

4. A Scots Executive Engineer

During winter one Scots Executive Engineer in Sind would confine himself to the roof of his bungalow with a large quantity of food and drinks and go on a drinking spree. He armed himself with a shotgun and did no office work. Once for fifteen days he was enjoying himself in this fashion, ignoring telegrams from his head office. Ultimately the Chief Engineer had to come down all the way from Karachi. He went upstairs unarmed and brough the Executive Engineer to his senses.

5. A novel method of disposal

A Collector in Sind had developed an ingenious method of quickly disposing of his files. On three days in a week he would accept all proposals put up by the office, while on the remaining three days he would reject all office proposals. But the days for acceptance or rejection of proposals were uncertain and he would change these days in an unpredictable manner, with the result that the office always remained alert.

Einstein's formula for success

Einstein is one of the greatest scientists the world has ever known. He had the unique genius of getting to the heart of any problem and suggesting the simplest possible solution. He wrestled with the most complex problems in physics but he used only paper, pencil, and the blackboard.

Once when he was asked what the secret of his achievements was, he replied, with characteristic simplicity and mathematical brevity:

S = X + Y + Z, where, S = Success, X = Hard work,

Y = Rest or Relaxation, Z = Keeping one's mouth shut.

This formula is universally valid.

Without hard work no one can achieve excellence in any field. Even a great batsman cannot afford to miss net practice before an important match.

Rest or relaxation is an equally essential requirement, as we have seen earlier. Einstein himself was fond of music. Once when he was greatly distressed and disappointed, as he found that his solution to a most complex problem in physics was wrong, he played the violin for several hours.

Z, that is silence, has great significance. Silence is golden, as the proverb goes. Silence makes us think deeply. It endows our mind with serenity. It gives us a sense of proportion. It can be creative. It is for this reason that Mahatma Gandhi used to observe silence one day in the week.

It should, however, be added here that executives must also develop the art of communication, because communication plays a vital role in the working of organisations. They must be able to listen to others, and also talk in a way that is easily understandable.

■ The secret of Japan's economic miracle

Japan's economic development during the last forty years is a miracle, unprecedented in world history. A nation which has only 0.3 per cent of the world's land, but has 3 per cent of the world's population, and is a poorly endowed with essential raw materials, produces 10 per cent of the world's Gross National Product. Considering the fact that Japan had been totally devastated in the Second World War, this is an awe-inspiring achievement, which provides an apt lesson for all developing countries which are waging a war against poverty.

One of the major factors contributing to this phenomenal success is continuous, lifetime training—which is not only technical or management training, but also ethical training.

The Japanese philosophy of lifetime training is explained in the following pages.

■ What is Zen Buddhism

This is a complex theme. Briefly, Zen means systematic training of the mind. It aims at disciplining the mind itself, to make it its own master. It is pre-eminently practical. It therefore lays great emphasis on manual work, cleaning, washing, and gardening. Zen has a unique approach to life and work.

Ten minutes and eighty years

A well-known story about the great Zen master, Hakuin Ekaku, illustrates how perfection in work is achieved. He had painted a magnificent picture of Daruma, the founder of the Zen sect. When he was asked how long it took him to complete the painting, he gave a puzzling reply: 'Ten minutes and eighty years.' This brief reply implies several things. First and foremost, it means that perfection is not easily attainable. Perfection demands lifelong study and practice. Secondly it emphasises the fact that even the last few minutes of work are invaluable. A finishing touch given in the last few minutes may enhance the beauty of the painting immeasurably. In a one-day cricket match even the last ball may decide the fate of the contest.

Every minute is important

We are however not aware of the critical importance of the time factor. For instance, employees would stop their work at 4.30 p.m. saying that the closing time (5 p.m.) is approaching. To the Zen way of thinking, this is totally unacceptable. Thirty minutes is a valuable chunk of time which cannot be just thrown away. Some important work can be done even during the last few minutes.

■ Continuous lifetime training in Japan

Swordsmanship, calligraphy and the performance of music have been by tradition the most highly respected arts in Japan. They demand constant practice and even an expert cannot afford to miss his daily practice. The Japanese believe that continuous training can lead to continuous improvement in performance. This concept of continuous training has been extended by them to industry. Everyone, from a sweeper to a managing director, must necessarily undergo regular training throughout his career.

■ The Zen philosophy versus the Confucian

Peter Drucker has discussed the Japanese approach to education very perceptively. He calls it the Zen approach, as opposed to the Western and the Chinese approach to education, which he calls the Confucian approach.

According to the Zen approach, the purpose of training is continuous improvement in performance. Everybody can improve his work throughout his career by continuous training. This leads to self-development, and the improvements achieved bring lasting satisfaction. On the other hand, the Confucian approach holds that the aim of training is to qualify the trainee for a more important job. In other words, training is for promotion and higher pay.

The Confucian approach is inferior to the Zen approach for several reasons. It focuses attention on status, wages, and other benefits rather than on excellence in work. The fact that there is both need as well as scope for improving on the present performance is thus lost sight of. And if the training is not followed by promotion quickly enough, there is frustration and resentment. The Zen approach stresses the obligation to improve on the present performance without expecting any tangible material return. When a person improves his performance, it can give him immense satisfaction. There is in everyone the inherent urge to attain excellence in one's own field. The Zen approach satisfies this urge. It also strengthens the urge for perfection. It points out that even the sweeper can improve on his performance. This is beneficial to him as well as to the factory where he is employed.

■ The training programme

Training sessions in Japan are held every week as part of the regular factory schedule. There is no teacher. The training programme is conducted by the supervisors, and everyone connected with the department, including even the sweepers, participates. The focus is not on any particular operation. The programme is designed to give an understanding of the whole process, the entire activity of the department. An accountant, for instance, may be required to study a number of related topics, such as workstudy and quality control.

Such a training programme gives the trainee a deeper understanding of the working of the department and broadening his outlook. It creates an attachment for the department and the job, and it strengthens the desire to learn and improve on one's performance.

The entire group becomes more enthusiastic, more receptive to new ideas. Any resistance to change and to innovation disappears. On the contrary, there develops a strong urge to be up-to-date. The introduction for new processes, methods or machines, stimulates the creative spirit. The feeling of monotony and boredom on the shop floor is thus dispelled.

The training programme is a co-operative venture. It mobilizes the knowledge and experience of the entire team. It brings about greater cohesion in the group and develops team spirit. The tendency to avoid work by saying, 'this is not my job', is discouraged. There is instead an eagerness to shoulder additional responsibility.

■ An exciting induction training programme for bank employees in Japan

■ An anthropologist becomes a trainee

Thomas Rohlen is a renowned anthropologist, who participated in a three-month induction training programme organised for new recruits by a leading bank in Japan. The following is a brief summary of an interesting article by Rohlen on this subject.

■ Army drill

After five weeks of preliminary training, the young recruits were taken to the training institute. They were given two simple uniforms, grey for study and white for athletics. The very first night they gathered at the institute, they practised military drill in preparation for a two-day trip to an army camp. In this camp they had to sweat their way over obstacle courses and had to undergo the army physical fitness test. It was explained to the trainees that a large organisation like the bank cannot work efficiently without strict army-like discipline.

Unpleasant things are part of life

The trainees later visited a museum dedicated to *Kamikazi*, the Japanese suicide pilots of World War II. The director of the museum, in his lecture to the trainees, emphasised two important truths. First, unpleasant things are a part of life and nothing significant can be achieved without suffering and sacrifice. Second, today's individualism ignores the interests of the community and degenerates into empty egoism.

■ Daily routine

The daily routine at the Institute was carefully organised. The day began with exercises and dormitory clean-up at 6.30 a.m. Each day involved 14 hours of supervised activity, with only Sunday as a holiday. Even the grooming of the trainees, their posture, and language were under observation. In each stairwell, a mirror was hung to remind the trainees of their appearance. The trainees spent one evening practising the correct way to bow. They also had to learn Zen meditation which is an arduous process.

The importance of co-operation was another major theme. The Japanese philosophy that even small things can be done neatly and properly with great benefit was continually emphasised. For instance, when the trainees left their slippers in a messy heap at the door of the lecture hall, the instructor took them to the door and showed how they should be lined up. 'Co-operation even in such small things helps everyone. A bit of forethought, a bit of self-control and a concern for others are all that is required', he said.

■ Begging for work

This was a very significant part of the training programme. The trainees were taken to a youth centre in rural Japan from where they were sent to a small town to beg for work. It was not easy to get work even without pay. Some worked in the fields, some sold toys, and some others delivered groceries.

This exercise was following by group discussions about the meaning and significance of work. The general conclusion was that the enjoyment of work has more to do with a person's attitude towards work rather than the kind of work itself. Work is intrinsically neither good nor bad, satisfying, or unsatisfactory. Whether a job will be a joy or drudgery depends upon one's outlook. This was the main lesson emerging from the training programme.

The trainees were also taught banking and related subjects. The importance of banking was repeatedly stressed. The basic message was: because the company serves the public interest, good workers are good citizens. Low interest rates are possible when banks are efficiently and carefully managed. And this helps everyone, businessman, consumer, and the nation.

■ Marathon walk

The last important event was the 25-mile marathon walk. This was a most arduous exercise. Its aim was to give the trainees a sense of confidence, that one can achieve the impossible if one is prepared to work for it.

The two-week training programme for women was differently organised. They were taught, apart from banking and other technical matters, that 'proper etiquette and polite language would make a woman cultivated, charming, and graceful, and thus a more attractive wife and an exemplary mother.'

According to the Industrial Training Association in Japan, one-third of all companies employing 1,000 or more people have introduced similar induction training programmes. And it must be said that they have produced excellent results.

■ Lesson for India

Such induction training programmes are unknown in India. And there is also no continuous lifetime training for employees as in Japan. In other words, there is no training and education for good work as in Japan. The result is that although lifetime employment is provided by government and other major organisations it has merely resulted in apathy and indifference in performance. Lifetime employment must go hand in hand with lifetime training for continuous improvement in performance.

CHAPTER 5

Time and energy management

Lost yesterday, somewhere between sunrise and sunset, two golden hours, each set with 60 diamond minutes. No reward is offered, for they are gone forever.

—*Horace Mann*

"60 diamond minutes"

■ The art of working

Work always involves some expenditure of time and energy. If this expenditure proves to be fruitful, work becomes a matter of joy and it inspires the individual to work more, to work better. Work demands some discipline, as desultory work is unrewarding. On the other hand, a job well done, howsoever small, benefits all, the individual, his organisation, and the nation. A good piece of work thus becomes its own reward. This chapter explains some essential aspects of the art of working–using one's time and energy most effectively. This chapter will mostly deal with time management by the executive.

■ Time is the scarcest, irreplaceable, and indispensable resource

The executive's most valuable resource is time. Without time, no work can be done. It is indispensable for every piece of work. The executive can work only for a limited number of hours per day. Time is thus the scarcest resource at his disposal. The supply of time is totally and absolutely fixed. It cannot be augmented. And time lost is lost for ever. It cannot be regained, recovered, or replaced by something else. It can not be accumulated like money. Time is thus the most valuable resource the executive possesses. And yet it is wasted in innumerable ways. Executives find it difficult to manage their own time independently. It is often said that executives have no time of their own. Their time is consumed by others, bosses, subordinates, customers, trade union officials, visitors, and unforeseen events. The effectiveness of an executive ultimately depends upon his time management.

■ Time and energy management

All clock hours are identical in the mechanical sense of the term. But the time when, for instance, one has a splitting headache, is of no use. It becomes an unbearable burden. It is therefore more appropriate to think in terms of time and energy management. The time that matters is the time when one has some energy for work.

■ Time is equitably distributed, but energy and talent are not

For everyone the day consists of twenty-four hours, although the life span may vary from individual to individual. On the other hand, all are not equally energetic. Human energy also fluctuates over time. One may be energetic today, while listless tomorrow. Similarly, all are not endowed with equal talent. It is said that Bertrand Russell's mind used to work with the velocity of light. Clement Attlee made important decisions with great rapidity. At the other extreme there are people for whom even simple arithmetic is a bugbear.

■ One does not necessarily age chronologically

Another peculiarity of energy is that one may be more energetic at fifty than at forty. It is often found that older people work with greater concentration and vigour than many young people. Voltaire, for instance, wrote his masterpiece, *Candide,* when he was sixty-four years old.

■ Punctuality is the first rule of time management

The importance of this principle cannot be overemphasised. It is obvious, but in practice it is seldom respected. As a result of unpunctuality, millions of hours are lost every day. An executive who wants to improve his own time management must aim at strict punctuality in the first place. This is bound to have great impact on the punctuality of his subordinates.

In the famous Japanese firm, Matsushita, most of the people in the managerial cadre come to office at least twenty minutes before the starting time. Other employees naturally follow their example.

■ An illustration of an ideal time manager

Peter Drucker has given a vivid illustration of an accomplished time manager.

'One of the most accomplished time managers I have ever met was the president of a big bank with whom I worked for

Punctuality by the management affects the general staff

two years on top-management structure. I saw him once a month for two years. My appointment was always for an hour and a half. The president was always prepared for the sessions—and I soon learned to do my homework too. There was never more than one item on the agenda. But when I had been in there for an hour and twenty minutes, the president would turn to me and say, 'Mr. Drucker, I believe you'd better sum up now and outline what we should do next'. And an hour and thirty minutes after I had been ushered into his office, he was at the door shaking my hand and saying good-bye.'

This simple example brings out effectively the following principles of time management.

(i) There is a natural limit to how long one can listen, speak, or discuss with rapt attention. This limit is called the span of attention. Generally the span of attention is of about ninety minutes.

(ii) If the time is to be used fully, there should be no interruptions. In this illustration the bank president had given strict instructions to his secretary not to put anyone through while the meeting was going on. On no account was the meeting to be disturbed. This facilitated concentration.

(iii) There was only one item on the agenda, which ensured thorough discussion. It is wasteful to discuss many topics cursorily.

(iv) The discussion was summarised at the end, which ensured perfect understanding of the conclusions reached. Summing up concisely and clearly is in itself an art.

(v) The agenda for the next meeting was decided, which facilitated, the home work of both, the bank president and the consultant. This is planning.

■ The need to take a time-log

Executives often feel frustrated as they are overburdened and have no time for really important work. The basic reason is their failure to manage time effectively. They just fritter away their time and energy on matters that arise in the course of the day.

The first step for improving time management is to take a time-log —an accurately maintained record of how one actually spends one's time. Memory is not reliable for this purpose. Only a correctly maintained record would show how time is spent on different activities, such as answering telephone calls, personal discussions, visitors, customers, reading, instructing, and writing or dictating, and so on.

The next step is to analyse the record to find out where the time really goes. The time-log will also indicate how discretionary time can be consolidated. Discretionary time is the time over which the executive has full control. If, for example, the executive sees visitors throughout the day, he may have a few minutes between two meetings which are of no use for important work. But he can reschedule the appointments in such a way that he has at least one uninterrupted hour in the morning, as well as in the afternoon. This is consolidation of discretionary time, when the executive can do his most important work undisturbed.

■ Identification of time wasters

The time-log will also be useful for deciding

- who are the main time wasters;
- whether important work is given adequate time at the appropriate hours;
- ways and means for improving time management such as rescheduling visiting hours;
- whether subordinates have to wait for instructions.

■ It is equally essential not to waste the time of subordinates

It is a bad practice to keep subordinates waiting for long, which is very frustrating for them. If, for example, the mail is sorted out late in the afternoon, the staff may have to work late in the evening to dispose of urgent matters.

■ Organisational objectives must be correctly established – a complex and time-consuming task

Time management is a means to an end —the attainment of well-defined objectives. Defining the objectives of a business is a difficult and demanding task which depends upon market research, reflection, vision, and discussion with all concerned. This cannot be achieved hurriedly. It is essential to provide adequate time for this formidable task. The decisions taken will make or mar the future of the organisation.

■ In his day-to-day work the executive should aim at doing the right thing in the right manner at the right time

Consider the issue of an invitation card for a very important function. First, the text must be finalised, and then printed accurately and attractively. And the invitations must be posted well in advance before the function.

A typical case may be mentioned here. For a very important function arranged at a short notice by a well-known firm, the invitation card was printed overnight as it had to be posted the next morning. But when it was shown to the chairman he was greatly upset as he found the wording inappropriate. The cards had to be reprinted with great haste and at considerable additional cost. And possibly some of the invitations did not reach in time.

■ Long-term as well as short-term (daily) planning is essential for the best use of time — that is for success

Konosuke Matsushita decided in 1956 that the company's sales should be increased from 20 billion Yen to 80 billion Yen in five years.

Though, on the face of it, it appeared to be an impossible task, it was in fact achieved in four years. The target was broken down from each year, month, and day for each division and each salesman. This is an exercise in long-term as well as short-term planning. Time devoted to planning can prove to be a most valuable investment. One top-ranking American firm has introduced a 'Weekly Work Sheet' which must be completed by the salesmen, giving the names of the people they plan to see next week. An *advance* copy of this Work Sheet is required to be sent to the head office. This sheet has proved to be a most effective tool for the success of the firm.

■ Trying to do too many things at a time is wasteful

The number of important tasks that can be handled at one time is strictly limited, as time is limited, and attention cannot be switched quickly from one subject to another. If the available time is spread over numerous tasks in small chunks, no progress can be made and all the time is wasted.

After all, even the best surgeon can perform only a limited number of major operations in a day.

The tasks must be selected carefully, taking into consideration their value, the time required for completion, and the time available. The temptation to please everyone must be resisted.

Trying to do too many things at a time

Dr. Francis Crick, a Nobel Laureate, uses a printed post card effectively to save time and energy.

How a Nobel Laureate saves his time

Dr. Crick thanks you for your letter but regrets that he is unable to accept your kind invitation to:

- ❑ send an autograph
- ❑ provide a photograph
- ❑ cure your disease
- ❑ be interviewed
- ❑ talk on the radio
- ❑ appear on TV
- ❑ speak after dinner
- ❑ give a testimonial
- ❑ help you in your project
- ❑ read your manuscript
- ❑ deliver a lecture
- ❑ attend a conference
- ❑ act as chairman
- ❑ become an editor
- ❑ write a book
- ❑ accept an honorary degree

■ Time should not be spent on unnecessary work

Some executives spend a good deal of their time in making unnecessary corrections to routine drafts put up by subordinates or rewriting their own letters, which are of minor importance.

Unnecessary corrections

During the Second World War, eminent university Professors had joined the civil service in the U.K. Once a Professor prepared a press note saying: 'We have now appointed a statistician in the department'. His boss was fond of correcting the drafts of his subordinates. He struck out the sentence and wrote instead, 'We have now created a statistical wing in the department'. 'When the Professor ruefully pointed out that one expert did not constitute a wing, the officer modified his own sentence by inserting the words 'the nucleus of'.

This is a wasteful exercise as it does not bring about any real improvement, but merely increases work and discourages the subordinates. The executive needs to have a sense of proportion.

■ Important tasks should be tackled when one's mind is fresh and vigorous

One of our High Commissioners in London used to work long hours, well past midnight. In the mornings he would attend to routine work such as checking log books for the fleet of cars maintained by the Embassy, which was really the work of an accountant. Late at night he would finalise important military contracts involving crores of rupees and concerned with the security of the nation. At the end of the day he would be fatigued and could not give these contracts the close attention they needed. These contracts were subsequently found to be defective and the nation had to suffer heavily.

■ Overwork can be harmful

Bagehot (Pronounce 'Badget'), the perceptive historian, has said that he knew many bankers in the city of London who went bankrupt because they worked ten or twelve hours a day. He adds that had they worked fewer hours they would have been rich.

The essential point is that there is a limit to the individual's capacity for work. Overwork creates a distaste for work which is then somehow managed in a slipshod manner. Important decisions are best made only when one can think effectively.

Why President Kennedy made some fatal decisions

Kennedy tried to develop a truly creative team. His decision making organisation was like a wheel, with himself at the hub. He used to participate in the discussions with great enthusiasm. To be at the hub of the wheel is not easy as it makes strenuous demands on the decision-maker. It appears that Kennedy made some momentous faulty decisions at times when he was totally exhausted. Tired and exhausted, he could not think with clarity and the meetings were dominated by CIA representatives, with unfortunate consequences.

■ The Pareto principle

According to this principle, eighty per cent of the results are due to twenty per cent of the causes. Attention could be focused on these twenty per cent causes most profitably.

In one factory, machine idle time was found to be abnormally high. There can be many reasons for this state of affairs, such as absenteeism, power shortage, no work, and shortage of materials. Analysis based on the Pareto principle showed that the main cause was shortage of materials. Once the cause was correctly identified, swift action could be taken and idle time was almost eliminated.

Prime Minister Attlee has stated this basic idea very perceptively in his characteristic way. 'When the logs are jammed in the river, one must begin by extricating one or two, in the hope that thereby the whole mass might move.'

■ Effective use of time depends upon the capacity for concentration

The capacity for concentration depends on the depth of interest in the subject. Concentration is also a matter of practice. Concentration further depends on the span of attention. Normally a person cannot listen to or speak attentively for more than ninety minutes at a time. Perfect work is the product of concentration. Swami Vivekananda mastered the four books of Euclid's geometry within twenty-four hours, as he had perfected the art of concentration.

■ Brooding leads to wastage of time and energy

Brooding is painful. It dissipates one's energy and enthusiasm. Regrets for past failures and mistakes are paralysing. Clement Attlee was a most effective decision-maker because once he made the decision carefully, he would never ask himself whether he had done the right thing as explained earlier. It takes one nowhere. The best course is to concentrate on the next job.

■ The time required for important tasks should be estimated liberally

It is a natural instinct to complete any important work, such as the drafting of a report or a research paper as quickly as possible, and accordingly the time requirements are estimated very economically. But as Murphy's law reminds us, 'everything takes longer than you think'. There are several reasons for it. As the work progresses, new difficulties may be encountered or new ideas suggest themselves. One may not be satisfied with the quality of work already done or one may be simply lacking in energy. The general rule is to estimate the time on a liberal basis for such tasks, so that disappointment for missing the deadline is avoided and a high quality of work is achieved.

■ As a corollary, simple tasks must be done quickly, without any prolonged deliberation

Questions such as the selection of stationery for office use should be decided quickly. Such decisions could even be left to an officer at a lower level. There is the well-known case of an executive who held several meetings to decide what type of sandwiches should be bought for the automatic vending machine proposed to be installed in the office.

■ Procrastination is wasteful

It entails delays and waste of time. It creates a feeling of uncertainty in the organisation. It can slow down the working of the entire organisation. For instance, delayed appointments of heads of public sector undertakings can lead to heavy losses. Procrastination may be the result of poor health, lack of confidence in one's judgement, or aiming at perfection, or a climate of uncertainty. Procrastination may be unavoidable in exceptional situations, but if it becomes habitual, it is a sure indication of the decay of the organisation.

■ The budgeted time should be made available in sufficiently large chunks

If, for instance, it is estimated that 24 hours are required to draft a report, it is no use setting aside only half-an-hour a day and completing the work in 48 days. No worthwhile work can possibly be done in half an hour. The time will be wasted in merely gathering the threads everyday. Similarly it is not desirable to work 12 hours a day and complete the report in only 2 days. It is difficult to work for 12 hours with concentration and the quality will suffer. The best plan would be to work 3 or 4 hours a day.

■ Interruptions must be strictly avoided

The time allotted for an important task must be uninterrupted, which alone can facilitate concentration. The quality of thinking and writing is governed by the degree of concentration achieved.

Procrastination is wasteful

Absorption in the theme has a marked impact on the quality of work.

■ As Churchill said, perfection is paralysis

No doubt adequate time must be provided for important work, but the pursuit of perfection could cause paralysis. After a certain stage the quest for further improvement can be a misguided venture, and in fact the quality may suffer. There is also the possibility that the work may never be completed.

■ The time budget must be sufficiently flexible

It is necessary to prepare a time budget, a plan of work, for the day, the week, and the month. But it must necessarily have some measure of flexibility. In any industrial organisation, an industrial relations problem for instance, can arise unpredictably and the executive must set aside other work to restore order and peace. Some unforeseen difficulties, problems, and accidental happenings recur from time to time which require prompt attention.

■ In exceptional situations, no action may save a lot of time and trouble

As the saying goes, some wounds heal themselves without any treatment. There are many situations when it is best to wait. Gobind Vallabh Pant used to dispose of his files very quickly. But a few he would keep back where he sensed that the issues raised therein would resolve themselves. Such an act requires insight and judgement.

■ Frequent emergencies are a symptom of poor management

An organisation where everything is urgent is probably poorly managed. (There are exceptions as in the case of the emergency ward in the hospital.) In an efficient organisation everything is pre-planned systematically and crisis situations are rare. On the other hand, in a poorly managed factory production may be frequently withheld for a variety of reasons.

■ The urgent is not always the important

If, for example, the office telephone is out of order, it must be got repaired as quickly as possible. This is an urgent requirement. But the preparation of the budget for the next year is a matter of great importance, which must be done with sufficient care. To do it hurriedly would be harmful.

■ Planned non-availability is essential for achieving concentration

As pointed out earlier, executives often have no time of their own. They are required to be available to others, subordinates, bosses, customers, and government officials at all times. They are talking on the phone endlessly and attending meetings and seminars. They are thus unable to concentrate on their main work, such as making important decisions or drafting important communications.

Some executives therefore prefer to work at home every morning for about two hours. They disconnect the telephone to avoid interruptions. Some others give strict instructions to their subordinates to ensure that they are not disturbed while they are engaged in some important work, on any account. A managing director of a big firm spends his weekend at the company's guest house at a nearby hill station, where he disposes of his work accumulated over the week. There is no one to disturb him. He has proved to be a very effective executive.

■ Essential information facilitates decision and action

In a hospital, for instance, admission to new patients can be granted without delay if accurate information regarding the availability of beds is readily available at the registration office at all times.

■ Excessive information can cause confusion and delay

Executives are now exposed to an overabundance of information as a result of the computer and the xerox machine. But excessive information cannot be digested easily. It can be a source of confusion and delays. Excessive information can be as blinding as excessive illumination. The quest for additional information, which can only lead to delays, must be curbed. Lee Iacocca has no computer terminal on his table, as he says that what the computer tells you is what somebody else has put in. And he adds that American managers do not know how to use the information available.

Excessive preoccupation with unimportant details is a source of confusion, uncertainty, and delays. It is precisely this mistake which President Carter used to make. He is described as a leaf man, one who was not satisfied with a view of the forest, or of even the trees, but he wanted to inspect every individual leaf.

Excessive information can be cofusing

He had thus no time for reflection and his judgement was clouded by the mountainous accumulation of facts and figures.

■ Time can be saved considerably by adopting the best possible means and methods

F.W. Taylor, the father of scientific management, raised the output of loading and unloading of pig iron from 12.5 tons per day to 48 tons a day by adopting the following formula:

- ❑ He selected the best man for the job.
- ❑ He worked out the best method of doing the job.
- ❑ He designed the equipment which was most suitable.
- ❑ He trained the man to work strictly according to the method.

The telephone, for example, can be used most effectively, instead of letters. It saves a good deal of time and effort. It is best suited for informal discussion. It is of course essential that important matters or decisions are recorded in writing.

■ Visible displays induce a sense of urgency, that the time is running out

For example, Mountbatten prepared for his staff and all the ministers and officials responsible for the arrangements for the partition of India, a small tear-off calendar giving the day of the month, printed underneath in bold type:

'X days left to prepare for the Transfer of Power.'

This reminded all his staff of the urgency of the task every day, every hour, and this most complex exercise was completed as scheduled.

■ Periodic assessment of progress can be helpful in achieving the target on time

After all, the ultimate objective of time management is to accomplish the task, say the construction of a building, by the scheduled date. It is necessary to assess the progress of work regularly and to take appropriate action if the project is not progressing as required.

Everybody, down to the lowest level, must be time conscious. It is however necessary to ensure that quality is not sacrificed at any stage to adhere to the time schedule.

■ Effective communication, brief, clear and practical, saves a good deal of time and effort

Instructions conveyed orally or in writing should not be ambiguous. Such instructions can lead to confusion or incorrect action. Instructions which cannot be put into practice create frustration and bitterness. A lengthy communication may prove to be boring and may not be read. President Kennedy is described as a Memo man who was fond of using the dictaphone. But his memos were mostly two or three line communications.

Collapse of the West Gate Bridge, Australia

This huge bridge over the River Yarra near Melbourne, Australia, collapsed on 15 October 1970. Thirty-five men were killed as a result of the collapse.

It happened in the morning when some thirty bolts were being removed in an attempt to deal with a buckle in some of the plates. The Commission of Enquiry, which thoroughly investigated the tragedy, could not conclusively establish who gave the instruction to remove the bolts and what exactly these instructions were. When the bolts were actually removed, the engineer concerned honestly believed that he was acting under the instructions of his superior, but since there was no written record, it was not possible to say whether the engineer acted correctly according to instructions. In such important matters, instructions have to be specific and clear cut and must be conveyed in writing.

■ Anticipatory action can save a lot of time, inconvenience and money

Preventive maintenance, for example, can reduce breakdowns of plant and machinery considerably. This ensures uninterrupted production and adherence to delivery schedules. All this improves the productivity and profitability of the firm.

■ Effective delegation is the key to effective use of time, talent and energy

Delegation is an art. Lord Curzon was the most imperial of all the Viceroys, a towering genius, with an encyclopaedic knowledge of India, endowed with a boundless capacity for work. He did everything himself. It was said, 'a sparrow can hardly twitter its tail in India without the action being attributed to direct orders issued by Lord Curzon'.

As a result, he was immensely overworked. Sometimes when he would work all night till five in the morning, his wife would beg him to come up to bed. He was officially admonished by the Secretary of State for excessive addiction to work.

Effective delegation is important

At the other extreme was Lord Dufferin, also an eminent Viceroy, who was known for extreme indolence. He even authorised his Private Secretary to forge his signature!

Field Marshal Montgomery was a superb organiser who left all his paperwork to his Chief of Staff. However, he himself drafted the battle plans in his own handwriting. This part of the work could not be delegated, as the master strategist alone could plan the battles.

Being relieved of all routine paperwork, he could concentrate on the conduct of battles. He was a strict disciplinarian. He would go to bed at 9 p.m. sharp and get up at 5 a.m. He was not to be disturbed at night on any account. When the great historic battle of El Alamein started with the booming of a thousand guns at 9.40 p.m., Montgomery was asleep. He could make everything crystal clear to all and he was supremely confident. He could be absolutely ruthless. When a military officer came very late for a meeting, he was sacked on the spot.

How to tackle a big task

Suppose a comprehensive manual is to be prepared for a large corporation. This is a daunting task, and one is apt to be frightened by its very magnitude.

But it must be kept in view that a cathedral cannot be built in a day. If one is patient, one plans systematically and works according to a well thought-out schedule, and the task becomes manageable. To start with one should concentrate one's attention on one chapter only, (forgetting other chapters for the time being). On its completion, the next chapter should be prepared, and so on. And one day one will be surprised to find that the task is completed.

The cluttered desk

A cluttered desk signifies an unsystematic approach to work. Papers are piled up gathering dust. They are mixed up and a good deal of time is wasted in searching out the required letters. An untidy desk is depressing. In the ideal situation the desk should be spotlessly clean and all papers and files should be kept on a nearby stand. There should be only one case on the desk at one time. This is essential for concentration. Only the essential stationery should be on the desk.

Effective use of the telephone

The telephone is a great device for saving time and energy, but in practice it often becomes a nuisance, as it wastes a good deal of time and seriously interrupts important work.

The following suggestions are made with a view to minimising the inconvenience caused by the telephone.

- Analysis of the calls received during one or two weeks will reveal (i) how much time was spent on unnecessary calls and (ii) how often important work was interrupted.
- Suitable hours can be fixed for placing and receiving calls. (This is ruled out in the case of hospitals or the police control room.)
- The secretary can be instructed to screen the calls.

- ❑ Before placing an outgoing call, one must be clear as to what exactly one has to say. And it must be said briefly and clearly.
- ❑ Small talk, if any, should be as brief as possible.
- ❑ The discussion should not be unduly prolonged.
- ❑ Ensure that there are no distractions while talking on the phone, such as shuffling of papers or talking to others.
- ❑ Important discussions should be immediately recorded in writing and a copy sent to the other person.

In one American firm the telephones are shut down for one hour every morning, with telephone operators taking messages during the hour. The better practice for the executive is to instruct the secretary not to put anyone through, while he is busy with some very important work.

■ How to make meetings productive

Meetings are generally considered to be boring and frustrating, consuming a lot of time and energy. They are generally too long and too many, and often ineffective and indecisive.

But meetings are unavoidable, and all that can be done is to make them more systematic and fruitful. They need to be planned carefully and conducted in a disciplined manner.

The following suggestions will be found useful for this purpose:

- ❑ Strict punctuality should be enjoined.
- ❑ The agenda and the notes should reach the participants well in advance.
- ❑ The agenda should be manageable.
- ❑ The first two or three items may be of a fairly simple nature. (This is to ensure a good start and if some members arrive late owing to some difficulties they should not miss important decisions.) The remaining items should be arranged in order of their importance.
- ❑ Wherever possible, the expenditure involved should be indicated against each item.
- ❑ In simple routine matters, the meeting may be held by circulating the relevant files.

❑ The number of participants should be restricted in the following manner:

(a) Invitees should be carefully selected.

Invitees to the meetings should be selected

(b) They should have the option not to attend if they do not want to participate in the discussion. The minutes should be sent to them for information.

(c) In certain types of meetings all the participants need not be present all the time. They can attend the meeting for discussion of the matters they are connected with. This can be easily arranged by telling the executive engineer, for instance, that his project will come up for discussion at such and such a time.

■ Time management is a national problem

Speed is of the essence in management. Economic development depends upon speedy execution of projects. Costs are related to the passage of time, that is, manhour, machinehour and moneyhour (interest and depreciation). It has been reported that delays in India in the execution of 58 projects have entailed a frightening costs overrun of Rs.15,000 crores. (*Times of India*, Bombay, 28 January 1988)

Delayed execution of projects entails further continuation of misery for the poor sectors of the community. The importance of time management cannot be overemphasised. Immediately after the revolution in Soviet Russia, Lenin said, 'The task that the Soviet Government must set the people in all its scope is – learn to work.'

Plan to develop the Russian work ethic

In 1920, A.K. Gastev, a poet as well as an industrial engineer, founded a Central Labour Institute to promote the scientific study of factory organisation.

A leaflet issued at this time to eliminate the organisational illiteracy of the Russian people makes interesting reading:

'Time! System! Energy!' What do these words mean?

Time

Measure your time, control it!
Do everything on time! Exactly, on the minute!
Save time, make time count, work fast!
Divide your time correctly, time for work and time for leisure!
Utilize your leisure so as to work better afterwards!

System

Everything according to plan, according to system!
A note book for the system. Order in your place of work!
Each must work according to plan.

Energy

Pursue your goal stubbornly!
Try hard. Don't retreat after failure!
Always finish what you have started!
Communist Americanism, realism and vigilance!

■ Failure of the plan

It appears that this plan to develop a vigorous work ethic was not effectively implemented, for the present-day Russian work ethic is lamentably ineffectual. Neglect of day-to-day work has become the order of the day with tragic consequences. For instance, a few years ago on a state farm, on two long holidays in May, the entire staff was dead drunk and the cows were not fed. In all over 200 cows died of starvation and food poisoning.

Today Soviet Russia is facing a grave economic crisis. Many Russians work poorly, shirk work and drink hard. Gorbachev has therefore been compelled to redefine socialism as 'from each according to his ability, to each according to his work'. All along he has been emphasising the dire need for *'working an extra bit harder.'*

■ Cost of time thefts

It has been estimated by Robert Half, President of an international recruiting firm, that 'time theft' involves a loss of 98 billion dollars annually for American industry. (Considering that India's GNP is about 180 billion dollars, this loss is more than 50 per cent of India's GNP.) It is estimated that the average weekly time theft by way of long lunches, personal work during office hours, coming late and leaving early, tardiness, etc., comes to 4 hours and 5 minutes! Such a survey is overdue in India.

Time theft

Dr. Skinner on how to write better letters and reports in less time and with less fatigue

Executives spend a good deal of their time and energy in writing notes, letters, and reports. They can save a good deal of their time if they follow B.F. Skinner's practice in this respect. Skinner is one of the greatest living psychologists, who developed one of the first teaching machines. Millions of copies of his novel *Walden Two* have been sold.

Skinner's formula

I write more slowly. Hence...

a) more economically. Details omitted if not relevant; superfluous adjectives dropped. (And I use 'notehand' abbreviations);
b) with less fatigue. I write more on a given point before escaping to something else;
c) more deliberately, with much more planning.

I write more clearly. Hence...

a) I reread, or otherwise use, my notes more readily;
b) I take pleasure in the sheer appearance of my notes and with this added reinforcement write more of them;
c) I make fewer mistakes. 'What is worth doing is worth doing well.'

At least I am kept from doing worthless things, and the energy I save may indeed mean that what I do, I am more likely to do well.

A very curious byproduct—I play the piano more slowly, with much more attention to accuracy, completeness, fingering.

CHAPTER 6

How to build an ideal organisation

The story of HAM

(The Honda of America Manufacturing, Inc. Plant)

Soichiro Honda got angry with workers who played baseball on the plant grounds, saying to himself, 'In collective bargaining, they complain about having to work too hard. But when it comes to playing baseball, they do it until they become completely exhausted, even though baseball does not bring a single yen to them. What kind of men are they?' But then he thought, 'I must recognise that man achieves the highest degree of efficiency when he plays. If someone says he works out of loyalty to the company, he is a damned liar. Everyone must work for himself. Even I work because I like working. *I must create a workshop where everybody will enjoy working.*'

Honda Motor, Tetsuo Sakiya

■ Historical background

In 1982 Honda became the first Japanese company to manufacture automobiles in the USA. Three years earlier it had started manufacturing motorcycles in America. Other Japanese automobile manufacturers were doubtful whether American workers were capable of meeting the high standards of precision expected of them. But this seemingly impossible task was superbly accomplished by Honda. Most of the newly recruited workers had farming backgrounds and it was doubtful whether they could work in a factory which imposed strict discipline. But under Honda management they were quickly transformed into a devoted, disciplined, and highly productive workforce. In the beginning, the morning warm-up exercises were a source of irritation, but now many voluntarily participate in this daily ritual.

Some eminent experts have argued that Japanese management cannot operate in the USA successfully. It is, therefore, very interesting to see how the Honda management has, almost without any resistance, introduced the Japanese style of management to American culture with great success.

■ Business is people

The basic Japanese philosophy is that management must endear itself to the employees. Newly recruited American workers were greatly impressed by the egalitarian atmosphere prevailing in the Honda factory. They were designated as 'associates' (and their foremen, 'production coordinators') which at once gave

Management must endear itself to the employees

them dignity and self-respect. All wear the same uniform right from the president to the worker. They have a common canteen and parking spaces are not reserved according to status. They are occupied on a first-come first-served basis. The offices are open, without any partitions. The egalitarian environment creates the feeling that everybody is important, which makes the organisation truly productive and creative.

Creating a workshop where everybody enjoys working

As Mary Parker Follett, a farsighted management philosopher, has said, 'What enhances self-respect of the individual, enhances his efficiency'. Honda treats its workers respectfully. They are called *associates* and not *workers* which is indeed most significant. The firm has full faith in the capabilities of the staff. Their views are considered with utmost respect. Initially, the lunch period was forty-five minutes but many workers (associates) wanted it to be reduced to thirty minutes which was, after putting the matter to vote, accepted.

Similarly as the plant was closed for several days on account of a severe storm, it was necessary to make good the loss of production either by working overtime or by working on Saturdays. The matter was again put to vote and it was decided to work every other Saturday. 'It is our belief that Honda should respect the judgement of our associates.' Such intangibles are more important than the fringe benefits, in creating an *esprit de corps*.

■ A non-union shop

A union does not exist at HAM and no lifetime employment is guaranteed by HAM. But HAM workers receive pay equal to that of unionised workers elsewhere. In Japan the normal practice is to promote people according to seniority, but Honda promotes people by merit, regardless of age. The accent is on youthfulness and excellent performance of work.

■ Training

In addition to the training programmes organised in America, workers and supervisors are sent to Japan for advanced training at considerable cost, ranging from $ 5,000 to $ 10,000 per person. But this has proved to be a valuable investment. On return, they train other workers. One lady metallurgist who was sent to Japan considers this to be 'the most rewarding experience of her life'. As she says, 'To be given the opportunity to observe some of the world's premier steel companies is a metallurgist's dream come true. I absorbed so much knowledge — things I never could learn in a class room or read in a book.'

■ Teamwork

As in all Japanese factories, Honda emphasises the importance of teamwork. 'Our job is everything' is the guiding principle. There is no job demarcation, as is the practice in America, with the result that workers are prepared to do any work and assist each other readily. They never say, 'this is not our job'. Work does not suffer if someone is absent. Job rotation is regular, so that boredom is dispelled.

The team leader is an ideal leader, who comes to his section thirty minutes before the starting time and ensures that tools, materials, and other prerequisites are available for the day's work, which is carefully planned. By his own thorough performance, the foreman sets an example and energises his teammates. He assists them, guides them, and encourages them in various ways. The emphasis is always on the quality of work.

Similarly, various types of internal training programmes are arranged for workers and team leaders so that there is continuous improvement in performance.

■ Quality — top priority

A few years ago a Japanese Professor wrote a book called *The Great American Disease* in which he pointed out that an American car cannot be sold in Japan unless it is given an additional coat of paint, so exacting are the expectations of the Japanese customer. Honda naturally insists upon the highest quality standards, which are never sacrificed. American management, as Deming has said, is dominated by numbers, Japanese management by quality. Every car goes through a series of rigorous inspections by about thirty people and even a minor blemish is promptly removed.

Quality versus quantity

The advantages of this stress on quality are immense. Workers feel proud about their cars as well as the firm. 'Since I started working here I notice with pride every Honda that goes by on the road', is a normal comment. The customers too are fully confident about the quality and performance of the car.

■ Basic philosophy

Some years ago, the great Soichiro Honda, founder of Honda, explained his philosophy. According to him, he owes his success to the confidence he has in each of his workers. It is these people who build Honda's superb machines.

His confidence in the workers is based on certain convictions. First he feels that every worker is the best worker as far as his own job is concerned, and further, he can think creatively if he is treated with respect and encouraged to think boldly, and even allowed to make mistakes. Without failures there is no success. As he puts it, 'Many people dream of success. To me success can be achieved only through repeated failure and introspection. In fact, success represents the one per cent of your work that results from the 99 per cent that is called failure.'

HAM encourages creative thinking and free discussion. The suggestions made by workers are considered carefully. Individual initiative is not curbed, but is positively encouraged. Honda is prepared to take risks involved in new ideas. Teamwork and individuality are blended to attain excellence in work, which is always pursued vigorously.

As in Japan, decisions are based on consensus in HAM. This has several advantages. The system ensures that questions are examined from different points of view and the human potential of the group, that is knowledge, creative, thinking, and practical experience, is fully used. The system strengthens team spirit and the people become closely involved in the affairs of the firm. The decisions are carried out with enthusiasm and vigour. The staff is thus encouraged to think freely, imaginatively, and boldly. The Honda World Idea Contest is designed to tap the potential creativity of the staff.

The Honda world idea contest

This contest is held in Japan once in two years. The object of the scheme is to stimulate workers' imagination, to encourage bold thinking and to make the fullest possible use of human talent, knowledge, and creativity in the organisation.

Hundreds of suggestions are received and after preliminary screening thirty ideas are selected and the participants given the funds for building small-scale models. From these thirty ideas, workers select two which are built as full-scale working models. The costs are paid by the company.

These two facility winners are then sent tò Japan to participate in the Honda World Idea Contest conducted at the company-owned amusement park and racing circuit. This in itself is a great honour. However, none of the ideas has been so far found to be marketable.

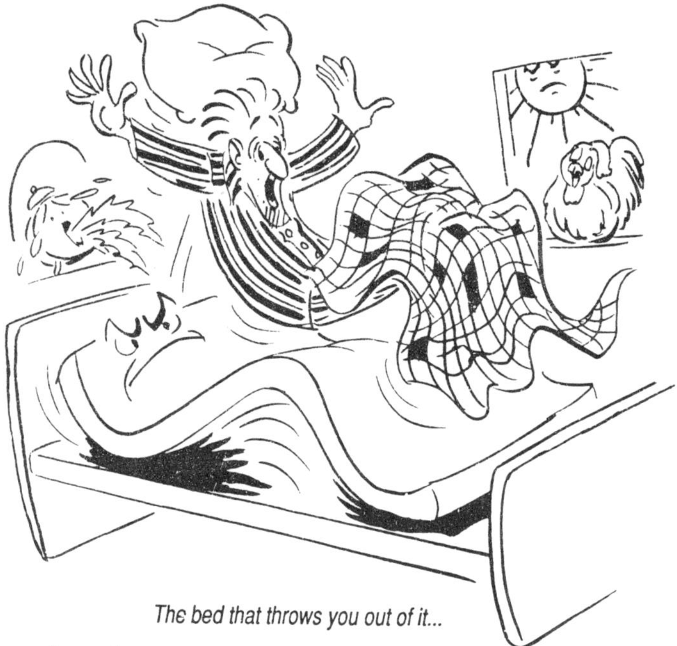

The bed that throws you out of it...

But the scheme serves its purpose. Many audacious ideas are put forth, such as 'a bed that throws you out of it if you do not get up on time', 'a fan-powered bicycle' and 'a motorcycle jacket that warms the rider on cold days with heat from the engine'. The spring of creativity never dries up at HAM.

■ The suggestion programme

While the Honda World Idea Contest is an ambitious long-term scheme, the Suggestion Programme may be described as a short-term one. But both are equally important. The great merit of the Suggestion Programme is that the suggestions received are examined promptly within a day or two. In May 1987, for example, 404 suggestions were implemented by the firm. And some of the suggestions have proved to be invaluable. For instance, a new solvent was developed for cleaning paint filters, which yielded an annual saving of $ 60,000.

The president of the company spends two or three days every month going round and informally discussing new suggestions with the workers. These visits have been found to be most fruitful. They energise the workers and boredom is dispelled.

■ N.H. circles (quality circles)

In HAM, quality circles are called the Now, Next, New Honda Circles. The working of these circles is more or less like the working of quality circles. The one major difference is that an N.H. Circle can start a project without the prior approval of management. Quality circles must be regarded as a revolutionary innovation, which effectively deal with the burning problem of workers' alienation.

The N.H. Circles hold their meetings after working hours and no overtime wages are paid. In 1987, about one-third of the workers were involved in this activity. The cost of the programme is over $ 1 million but it is justified by the gains that accrue. These programmes strengthen the urge for participation and are highly educative. Their contribution to higher productivity is immeasurable.

■ The voluntary involvement programme

It is a sort of merit-rating system in which points are awarded to workers for their performance and participation in activities like N.H. Circles. The names and photographs of the 100 top-ranking workers are displayed near the inside entrance of the factory. The prizes are generally not extravagant, but in exceptional cases, for outstanding performance over several years, the reward may be a brand new Honda automobile.

■ Continuous dialogue

The HAM workers' day begins with an informal meeting with their foreman before the shift begins. Under the Speak-out Programme the worker can air his grievances. All that he has to do is to fill in a form, which is given due consideration within 48 hours.

Another interesting feature of the communication system is called *Waigaya,* literally meaning chattering. It is something like brainstorming. *Waigayas* are regularly conducted at all levels in

HAM. It can be an informal meeting over lunch or a formally organised top-level management meeting. It has been found that these meetings are very useful for scrutiny and development of new ideas. As the authors of *A Passion for Excellence* point out, casual talk and naive listening can be highly rewarding.

The customer is the business

Peter Drucker has enunciated one basic business proposition. The purpose of a business is to create a customer. The customer is the business. After welcoming the new recruits the President of HAM tells them that he is not their boss. 'Our boss is our customers, and we must never forget that they come first.' To serve the customer best, the highest standard of quality and productivity must be first maintained. The higher productivity and quality of HAM can be attributed to the following factors:

The customer is the boss

■ Quality control

The basic ideas are derived from the teachings of the celebrated guru, Deming, who taught quality control to the Japanese and who is the originator of the concept of quality circles. In order to ensure strict quality control, Honda managers frequently go to the shop floor to identify the problems and to work out the necessary remedies.

■ Productivity-conscious staff

In Honda even after the recess bell goes, workers continue to work for thirty to fifty seconds, while in other American factories, the work is stopped instantly or even earlier.

It has been estimated that American workers steal an average of four hours and twenty-nine minutes a week — which amounts to six weeks in a year. There are no such time thefts in Honda.

The workers realise that everything can be improved from day to day. This makes work interesting and challenging. Small improvements can ultimately lead to spectacular changes.

■ Plant maintenance

The productive efficiency of the factory depends on the faultless working of plant and machinery. At 5.00 a.m. every day, ninety minutes before the first shift begins about forty maintenance engineers check the machinery thoroughly so that it works faultlessly. A computer system is introduced for routine maintenance, to achieve the goal of zero defects. If any breakdown cannot be repaired by the maintenance engineers, 'the company will fly in an expert from anywhere in the world within twenty-four hours'.

■ Just-in-time production

HAM stocks parts sufficient only for a few production hours or a few production days. Inventory costs are reduced to the minimum and floor space requirements are also restricted.

■ Marketing

Marketing is probably the toughest task faced by any firm. Marketing in America is quite different from marketing in Japan and initially Honda had to deal with marketing problems very carefully. The main objective was to pursuade the American public that Honda cars reflected high quality at a reasonable price. The selling points to be emphasised were: reasonable price, fuel efficiency, excellent quality, and prompt service.

An article in *Reader's Digest* titled 'From Japan: A "Clean Car" That Saves Gas' proved to be sensational. Thousands of copies of this article were sent out to automobile dealers throughout America.

As one American dealer observed, 'Honda's quality control for its factory paint has higher standards than the domestic auto makers. This eliminates a lot of grief, because a paint defect is the first thing a new-car buyer notices.'

Perhaps the most important selling point is the excellent after-sales service provided by Honda.